FOR MY MOM AND DAD, WHO HAVE ALWAYS
SHOWN ME WHAT HARD WORK MEANS.
THANK YOU FOR ALWAYS BELIEVING IN ME.
I'M SO PROUD TO CALL YOU MY PARENTS.

no-bake
TREATS

no-bake
TREATS

INCREDIBLE UNBAKED CHEESECAKES, ICEBOX CAKES, PIES AND MORE

julianne bayer

FOUNDER OF BEYOND FROSTING

PAGE STREET
PUBLISHING CO.

PAGE STREET
PUBLISHING CO.

First published in 2016 by
Page Street Publishing Co.
27 Congress Street, Suite 103
Salem, MA 01970
www.pagestreetpublishing.com

Distributed by Macmillan, sales in Canada by The Canadian Manda Group.

19   18   17   16   1   2   3   4   5

ISBN-13: 978-1-62414-246-8
ISBN-10: 1-62414-246-X

Library of Congress Control Number: 2016904297

Cover and book design by Page Street Publishing Co.
Photography by Julianne Bayer

Printed and bound in the United States

Page Street is proud to be a member of 1% for the Planet. Members donate one percent of their sales
to one or more of the over 1,500 environmental and sustainability charities across the globe who
participate in this program.

contents

seven
PUDDINGS AND PARFAITS

eight
HELPFUL TIPS AND TOOLS

introduction

Dessert is more than just a plate of pie, a spoonful of ice cream or a handful of cookies. Dessert is an experience, a memory created and a moment to be treasured and shared with others. And there is nothing more rewarding than taking the first bite of a dessert that you prepared.

My name is Julianne and I created Beyond Frosting, a blog about easy mouthwatering desserts for the novice chef. My goal is to take you on a dessert journey with me while inspiring you to get back in the kitchen.

Growing up, I always wanted to be in the kitchen and I've always had a sweet tooth. My grandma's nickname for me was Sugar, so it's no surprise that I run a business making desserts. I started blogging a few years ago when my passion for baking was reignited after taking cake decorating classes. What started out as a hobby quickly turned into a full-blown dessert obsession.

When it came time to decide on the topic for my cookbook, no-bake desserts were the first recipes to come to mind. When I first started my blog, I realized I had a love-hate relationship with cheesecakes. I love cheesecakes, but I hate to bake them. So I started making no-bake cheesecakes and have never looked back. I've evolved my knack for no-bake desserts into creating mouthwatering icebox cakes, ice creams, pies and more.

No-bake desserts are perfect for novice chefs looking to dip their toes in the water before diving in. There's not much guessing needed when it comes to no-bake desserts. With the easy-to-follow instructions in my book, you will find your way to dessert bliss.

More experienced bakers will also love this book because I've mixed simple no-bake concepts with more challenging elements and new flavor combinations. One thing is certain: Every recipe is fun and lends itself to putting your own personal touches to it. I look at every dessert as a creative opportunity for you to really let your personality shine through.

While creating this cookbook, I've discovered how much I truly love baking and learned how much I enjoy photography, which I've seen blossom the most throughout this experience. I've pushed myself out of my comfort zone to create the best recipes possible for you—and I'm sure you'll see that in the coming pages.

To help you get the most out of this book, I suggest flipping through my Helpful Tips and Tools chapter (page 205). I want you to be successful and experience the same enjoyment that I do when I create a dessert I never imagined I could.

I know you will love these recipes as much as I do. Happy no-baking!

Julianne Bayer

(one)

no-bake cheesecakes

I am so excited to share my no-bake cheesecakes with you. This was by far my favorite chapter to create, and that is not just because cheesecake is my favorite dessert. Cheesecakes are usually the first things that come to mind when you think of a no-bake dessert. When I share these desserts, most people can't believe they are actually from no-bake recipes. I really wanted to push the limits with the variety of cheesecakes found here. This chapter offers recipes from traditional cheesecakes such as apple or pumpkin to new flavors such as Blackberry White Chocolate Truffle (page 21), Monster Cookie Dough (page 25) and Lemon Macaroon (page 22). There is plenty of chocolate and coconut, fresh fruit and even a little bit of booze.

banana cream
PUDDING CHEESECAKE

If you had to choose between desserts, would you pick banana pudding or cheesecake?
I know, tough decision, right? Well, now you don't have to choose. My Banana Cream Pudding Cheesecake
combines cheesecake topped with fresh banana slices and vanilla pudding. It is finished with a layer of whipped
cream. You will need an extra-large fork to make your way through all of the the amazing layers in this cheesecake.
Be sure to pay attention to the steps necessary to create each layer of this wonderful dessert.
It may take a bit more time, but you'll be thankful after that first bite.

YIELD: 8 TO 10 SLICES

FOR THE PUDDING

2 large egg yolks, slightly beaten

⅓ cup (64 g) granulated sugar

2 tbsp (16 g) all-purpose flour

Dash of salt

1 ½ cups (355 ml) heavy whipping cream

½ tsp vanilla extract

FOR THE CRUST

11 oz (312 g) vanilla wafers (I use Nilla wafers)

8 tbsp (115 g) unsalted butter

FOR THE CHEESECAKE

16 oz (454 g) cream cheese, softened

½ cup (96 g) granulated sugar

2 tbsp (30 ml) heavy whipping cream

1 tsp vanilla extract

FOR THE TOPPING

2 cups (473 ml) heavy whipping cream

1 ½ cups (195 g) powdered sugar

2 whole bananas, sliced

6 to 8 vanilla wafers for garnish, crushed

FOR THE PUDDING

Measure out all of the ingredients for the pudding prior to starting. Place the egg yolks in a separate bowl. In a medium-size saucepan, add the sugar, flour and salt, and whisk to combine. Add the heavy whipping cream and vanilla extract, and heat the mixture on the stove top over medium-low heat. Whisk constantly to dissolve the dry ingredients into the cream mixture. After 5 or so minutes, once the mixture is warm (but not boiling), pour about ¼ cup (59 ml) of the cream mixture into the egg yolks and whisk vigorously to temper. Immediately pour the egg yolks into the saucepan and continue whisking over medium-low heat to prevent the eggs from cooking. Whisk until the pudding starts to thicken. Once the mixture is thick and bubbly, remove it from the heat.

Strain the pudding through a fine sieve into a medium-size bowl. This step is optional, but it will help catch any lumps of ingredients that did not get blended. Immediately cover the top of the pudding with clear plastic wrap (directly on the surface of pudding), and poke a few holes with a toothpick. Allow the pudding to cool for 30 minutes at room temperature, and then refrigerate for 2 hours until the pudding is cold.

FOR THE CRUST

Prepare a 9-inch (23-cm) springform pan by lightly greasing the edges of the pan with cooking spray, and then wiping gently with a paper towel. Grind the wafers into fine crumbs using a food processor or blender. In a microwave-safe bowl, microwave the butter for 45 to 60 seconds until the butter is melted. In a separate medium-size bowl, pour the melted butter into the cookie crumbs and stir until there are no dry crumbs left. Pour the crumbs into your springform pan and press firmly into the bottom to create a thick crust.

FOR THE CHEESECAKE

Beat the cream cheese on medium-high speed for 2 to 3 minutes until it's light and fluffy. Slowly add the granulated sugar into the cream cheese while continuing to beat the mixture, scraping down the bowl as needed. Next, add the heavy whipping cream and vanilla extract. Beat until the filling is smooth and creamy. Pour the cheesecake filling into the prepared pie crust, cover and refrigerate for 2 hours.

(continued)

FOR THE TOPPING

Prepare the whipped cream by placing the mixing bowl and whisk attachment in the freezer for 5 to 10 minutes to chill. Pour the heavy whipping cream into the chilled bowl and use an electric mixer to beat the heavy cream on medium-high speed until the cream gets bubbly. Slowly add the powdered sugar and continue beating on high speed until stiff peaks form. Separate out 1 ¼ cups (296 ml) of the whipped cream for piping an edge on cake.

To assemble the cheesecake, slice the bananas about ¼-inch (0.5-cm) thick. Start by aligning them on the outside of the cheesecake and work your way in toward the middle. Pour the chilled pudding over the top of the sliced bananas and smooth out with a spatula. Add the whipped cream over the top of the pudding and spread smoothly. Use the prepared whipped cream to pipe a border along the top of the cheesecake. Garnish with crushed vanilla wafer cookies. This cake must be refrigerated for another 2 to 4 hours before serving to allow all of the ingredients to set properly.

ultimate oreo
BIRTHDAY CAKE CHEESECAKE

Who needs a regular birthday cake when you can have 3 layers of amazingness! The bottom layer is a cake batter cheesecake stuffed with Oreos; I prefer to call it an Oreo cake batter cheesecake. The middle layer is plain cake batter cheesecake, and the top layer is a light and fluffy chocolate mousse. To say I am obsessed with this cheesecake would be an understatement. Each layer is unique. It may seem like a lot of work, but the bottom 2 layers of cheesecake are made at the same time, and then divided, so one has Oreos and one does not. You might even want to try using Birthday Cake Oreos, but who am I to tell you your Oreo business? You will need either 1 family-size (19-oz [541-g]) or 1 ½ regular-size (14-oz [405-g]) packages for this recipe.

I made this in an 8-inch (20-cm) springform pan instead of 9-inch (23-cm) because I wanted each layer to be nice and tall. You can certainly use a different size springform pan, but you might have thinner layers. Either way, you can't go wrong.

YIELD: 8 TO 10 SLICES

FOR THE CRUST

1 (19-oz [541-g]) package Oreos (or similar chocolate sandwich cookie)

8 tbsp (115 g) unsalted butter

½ cup (113 g) sprinkles

FOR THE CHEESECAKE

20 oz (567 g) cream cheese, softened

2 tbsp (30 ml) heavy whipping cream

¼ cup (48 g) granulated sugar

½ cup (65 g) dry vanilla cake mix

1 tsp vanilla extract

¼ cup (57 g) sprinkles

10 Oreos, crushed

FOR THE FILLING

4 oz (113 g) cream cheese

1 ½ cups (355 ml) heavy whipping cream

1 cup (130 g) powdered sugar

2 tbsp (14 g) cocoa powder

½ tsp vanilla extract

FOR THE TOPPING

¾ cup (177 ml) heavy whipping cream

½ cup (65 g) powdered sugar

5 Oreos, crushed

1 tbsp (19 g) sprinkles

FOR THE CRUST

Prepare an 8-inch (20-cm) springform pan by lightly greasing the edges of the pan with cooking spray, and then wiping gently with a paper towel. Grind the package of cookies into fine crumbs using a food processor or blender. In a microwave-safe bowl, microwave the butter for 45 to 60 seconds until the butter is melted. In a separate medium-size bowl, pour the melted butter into the cookie crumbs and stir until there are no dry crumbs left. Lastly, fold in the sprinkles until they are well incorporated. Pour the crumbs into your springform pan and press firmly into the bottom and up the sides (to the top) to form the crust. Set aside.

FOR THE CHEESECAKE

Using a medium-size bowl, beat the cream cheese and heavy whipping cream on medium-high speed for 3 to 4 minutes until it's light and fluffy, scraping down the sides of the bowl as needed. Add the sugar, dry cake mix and vanilla extract, and continue beating for 2 to 3 minutes until all of the ingredients are well incorporated. Divide the cream cheese in half. In one bowl, mix the sprinkles into the cream cheese and set aside. In another bowl, add the crushed Oreos and mix into the cream cheese until well combined. Set both bowls aside.

(continued)

FOR THE FILLING

In a large mixing bowl, beat the cream cheese at low speed for 30 seconds with the whisk attachment to eliminate any lumps. Increase the speed to medium and slowly add the heavy whipping cream, about ¼ cup (59 ml) at a time. The idea is to slowly add the whipping cream so that the cream cheese will not be lumpy. It should have a liquid consistency. Once all of the heavy cream has been added, increase the speed to high until the mixture becomes bubbly. Slowly add the powdered sugar, cocoa powder and vanilla extract, and continue beating until stiff peaks form.

To assemble the cheesecake, carefully spread the Oreo cheesecake filling into the prepared crust as your bottom layer. Use a knife to spread it evenly to the edges. Next, evenly spread on the sprinkles cheesecake filling. Finally, complete the cheesecake by spreading the chocolate mousse filling over the cheesecake layers. The cheesecake must be refrigerated for 4 hours to allow each layer to set. You can add the whipped cream topping at this point or prepare it right before serving.

FOR THE TOPPING

Chill your mixing bowl and whisk attachment in the freezer for 5 to 10 minutes. Pour the heavy whipping cream into the chilled bowl and use an electric mixer to beat the heavy cream on medium-high speed until the cream gets bubbly. Slowly add the powdered sugar and continue beating on high speed until stiff peaks form. Remove the springform pan edge and use a large star tip to pipe the whipped cream on the outside edges of the cheesecake. Garnish the top of your cheesecake with the crushed Oreos and sprinkles.

blackberry white chocolate
TRUFFLE CHEESECAKE

This cheesecake's filling is a combination of white chocolate, cream cheese and marshmallow crème. In each layer there is a swirl of fresh blackberry filling. The result is an ultralight cheesecake with a hint of sweetness and a contrast of tart blackberries. If there is one thing you need to know here, it is that you need to use high-quality white chocolate because it will impact the texture of the cheesecake. It should be nice and smooth before adding it to your batter.

YIELD: 8 TO 10 SLICES

FOR THE CRUST

2 cups (180 g) graham cracker crumbs

8 tbsp (115 g) unsalted butter

¼ cup (55 g) light brown sugar

FOR THE CHEESECAKE

10 oz (284 g) white chocolate chips

1 cup plus 5 tbsp (311 ml) heavy whipping cream, divided

16 oz (454 g) cream cheese, softened

7 oz (198 g) marshmallow crème

½ cup (65 g) powdered sugar

3 oz (85 g) blackberries

FOR THE TOPPING

¾ cup (177 ml) heavy whipping cream

½ cup (65 g) powdered sugar

8 to 10 blackberries for garnish

FOR THE CRUST

Prepare a 9-inch (23-cm) springform pan by lightly greasing the edges of the pan with cooking spray, and then wiping gently with a paper towel. Before measuring, grind the graham crackers into fine crumbs using a food processor or blender. In a microwave-safe bowl, microwave the butter for 45 to 60 seconds until the butter is melted. In a separate medium-size bowl, pour the melted butter over the graham cracker crumbs and brown sugar, and stir until there are no dry crumbs left. Pour the crumbs into your springform pan and press firmly into the bottom and up the sides of the pan to form the crust. Refrigerate the crust until the filling is ready.

FOR THE CHEESECAKE

In a microwave-safe bowl, combine the white chocolate with 5 tablespoons (74 ml) heavy whipping cream, and microwave in 30-second increments, stirring each time until the chocolate is melted and smooth. I suggest microwaving at 50 percent power, which helps prevent the white chocolate from seizing. Allow the chocolate to cool. In a medium-size bowl, beat the cream cheese on medium-high speed for 2 to 3 minutes until it's light and fluffy. Next, pour the melted white chocolate into the cream cheese, and blend until well incorporated. Lastly, add the marshmallow crème and continue beating until well mixed. Set aside.

Prepare the whipped cream by chilling your mixing bowl and whisk attachment in the freezer for 5 to 10 minutes. Pour the remaining 1 cup (237 ml) of heavy whipping cream into the chilled bowl and use an electric mixer to beat the heavy cream on medium-high speed until the cream gets bubbly. Slowly add the powdered sugar and continue beating on high speed until stiff peaks form. Fold the whipped cream into the cream cheese mixture until it is well blended. Your cheesecake filling will be divided into thirds.

Use a food processor to blend the blackberries until you get a liquid consistency. To build your cheesecake, pour ⅓ of the cheesecake filling into the pie crust and smooth out with a spatula. Drizzle ⅓ of the blackberry juice over the cheesecake and gently swirl it into the cheesecake with a knife or a spoon. Repeat these steps 2 more times. Cover and refrigerate for 6 to 8 hours; overnight is best.

FOR THE TOPPING

Combine the whipping cream and powdered sugar as described above to prepare a second batch of whipped cream. Remove the springform pan edge and use the prepared whipped cream to pipe a border along the top edge of the cheesecake. Garnish with additional blackberries.

lemon macaroon CHEESECAKE

My Lemon Macaroon Cheesecake is a bit outside of my comfort zone, and for that reason I am absolutely in love. Lemon is not my typical go-to flavor, so when I created such a decadent dessert using lemon, it made me especially proud. This coconut-filled cheesecake is topped with a layer of lemon curd and a generous helping of whipped cream. While I was shopping, I found some large flaked coconut that was lightly toasted—the perfect garnish for this cheesecake. If you can't find that, then go ahead and use shredded coconut. It's up to you if you want to toast it or not, but that would require you to turn on your oven. Make sure to cut yourself a big slice of this cheesecake when it's ready!

YIELD: 8 TO 10 SLICES

FOR THE CRUST

1 (16-oz [470-g]) package vanilla sandwich cookies such as Golden Oreos

6 tbsp (86 g) unsalted butter

FOR THE FILLING

3 tbsp (34 g) melted white chocolate

24 oz (680 g) cream cheese, softened

½ cup (96 g) granulated sugar

1 cup (76 g) shredded sweetened coconut

10 oz (284 g) lemon curd

FOR THE TOPPING

1 ½ cups (355 ml) heavy whipping cream

¾ cup (98 g) powdered sugar

½ cup (38 g) shredded, or lightly toasted large flaked coconut

FOR THE CRUST

Prepare a 9-inch (23-cm) springform pan by lightly greasing the edges of the pan with cooking spray, and then wiping gently with a paper towel. Grind the cookies into fine crumbs using a food processor or blender. In a microwave-safe bowl, microwave the butter for 45 to 60 seconds until the butter is melted. In a separate medium-size bowl, pour the melted butter into the cookie crumbs and stir until there are no dry crumbs left. Pour the crumbs into your springform pan and press firmly into the bottom and up the sides of the pan to create a thick crust.

FOR THE FILLING

To melt, microwave the white chocolate in a microwave-safe bowl in 15-second increments, stirring each time until the chocolate is melted and smooth. I suggest microwaving at 50 percent power, which helps prevent the white chocolate from seizing. Once melted, stir it until it's smooth and set aside. Allow the chocolate to cool. Beat the softened cream cheese on medium-high speed for 2 to 3 minutes until it's light and fluffy. Slowly add the sugar into the cream cheese and continue beating until the sugar is incorporated, scraping the bowl as needed. Add the melted white chocolate and shredded coconut, and beat the mixture at a high speed for 60 to 90 seconds to create a nice and airy filling. Pour the cheesecake filling into the prepared crust and spread evenly with a spatula. Spread the lemon curd over the top of cheesecake layer.

FOR THE TOPPING

Place the mixing bowl and whisk attachment in the freezer for 5 to 10 minutes to chill. Pour the heavy whipping cream into the chilled bowl and use an electric mixer to beat the heavy cream on medium-high speed until the cream gets bubbly. Slowly add the powdered sugar and continue beating on high speed until stiff peaks form. Add a nice thick layer of whipped cream atop the cheesecake. Garnish the top with large, flaked pre-toasted coconut or shredded coconut. Cover the pan with foil and refrigerate for 4 to 6 hours to allow to set.

monster COOKIE DOUGH CHEESECAKE

This recipe combines my love for cookie dough and my noticeable obsession with cheesecake. The crust-to-filling ratio is especially important for this cheesecake. Too much crust and you don't get enough of the filling. Not enough crust? You are left wanting more. Good thing I have solved the equation for you.

This cheesecake can also be made ahead of time and frozen! Just thaw it in the refrigerator overnight. Here is the most important tip, though: Don't add the M&M topping until you are ready to serve. The candy coating will start to melt when it comes in contact with any moisture. One last thing: If you don't have a springform pan, try making this in a 9-inch (23-cm) square pan instead and cut into bars. As with any no-bake cheesecake, be sure you allow enough time for the filling to set before serving.

YIELD: 10 TO 12 SLICES

FOR THE CRUST

8 tbsp (115 g) unsalted butter

½ cup (96 g) granulated sugar

¼ cup (50 g) light brown sugar

1 cup (180 g) creamy peanut butter

½ cup (62 g) all-purpose flour

1 tsp vanilla extract

2 cups (161 g) old-fashioned quick oats

¾ cup (135 g) M&M's or similar candy

½ cup (90 g) mini-chocolate chips

FOR THE CHEESECAKE

1 ½ cups plus 2 tbsp (385 ml) heavy whipping cream, divided

¾ cup (98 g) powdered sugar

12 oz (340 g) cream cheese, softened

¼ cup (48 g) granulated sugar

1 tsp vanilla extract

1 cup (180 g) mini-chocolate chips

FOR THE TOPPING

¾ cup (177 ml) heavy whipping cream

¼ cup (33 g) powdered sugar

2 tbsp (22 g) creamy peanut butter

1 cup (180 g) M&M's or similar candy

FOR THE CRUST

Line the bottom of a 9-inch (23-cm) springform pan with parchment paper. The paper can be higher than the edges; just be certain the bottom is tightly secured to the springform edge of the pan. Lightly grease the edges of the pan with cooking spray, and then wipe gently with a paper towel.

Soften the butter in the microwave for 10 to 15 seconds. In a medium-size bowl, combine the softened butter, sugar and brown sugar, and beat at a medium speed until well combined. Add the peanut butter and mix until well blended, scraping down the sides of the bowl as needed. Once combined, add the flour and vanilla extract, mixing just until the flour starts to incorporate. Slowly add the oats, 1 cup (81 g) at a time. The dough will start to thicken but continue mixing until combined. Fold the M&M's and mini-chocolate chips into the dough with a spatula or your hands so as not to crush the M&M's. Press the cookie dough into the bottom of the springform pan to create the crust.

FOR THE CHEESECAKE

Prepare the whipped cream first by placing the mixing bowl and whisk attachment in the freezer for 5 to 10 minutes to chill. Pour 1 ½ cups (355 ml) of heavy whipping cream into the chilled bowl and use an electric mixer to beat the heavy cream on medium-high speed until the cream gets bubbly. Slowly add the powdered sugar and continue beating on high speed until stiff peaks form. Set the whipped cream aside.

Beat the cream cheese on medium-high speed for 2 to 3 minutes until it's light and fluffy. Slowly add the sugar into the cream cheese while beating the mixture. Next, add the remaining 2 tablespoons (30 ml) of heavy whipping cream and the vanilla extract. Beat until the filling is smooth and creamy, scraping the bowl as needed. Fold the mini-chocolate chips into the cream cheese mixture.

(continued)

Slowly add the prepared whipped cream into the cream cheese mixture, folding over and over with a spatula until the whipped cream is well combined. Pour the filling into the prepared crust and smooth the top with a spatula. Before placing the cheesecake in the refrigerator, gently run a flat-edged knife around the edge to help release it slightly from the edges of the pan. This will make it easier to remove the edges of the pan without tearing into your cheesecake. Cover the pan with foil and refrigerate for 4 to 6 hours.

FOR THE TOPPING

Combine the whipping cream and powdered sugar as described above to prepare a second batch of whipped cream. Remove the springform pan edge and use a large star tip to pipe the whipped cream on the outside edges of the cheesecake.

Microwave the creamy peanut butter for 10 to 15 seconds and drizzle it over the edges of the whipped cream border. Prior to serving, garnish the top with additional M&M's. To serve, cut into the cheesecake with a sharp knife, and clean the knife after each cut.

blueberry crumble
CHEESECAKE

What is your favorite part of a muffin? For me, it's always the top of the muffin: I go crazy for streusel and crumble toppings. My Blueberry Crumble Cheesecake is a tribute to my fellow crumble lovers In this cheesecake, the buttery streusel topping and a thick graham cracker crust offset the tangy blueberry cheesecake filling. Those who have tried this recipe tell me they can't get enough of the topping.

YIELD: 8 TO 10 SLICES

FOR THE CRUST

2 cups (180 g) graham cracker crumbs

¼ cup (50 g) light brown sugar

6 tbsp (86 g) unsalted butter

FOR THE CHEESECAKE

1 cup (237 ml) heavy whipping cream

½ cup (65 g) powdered sugar

4 oz (113 g) white chocolate

16 oz (454 g) cream cheese, softened

½ cup plus 1 tbsp (108 g) granulated sugar, divided

2 tbsp (14 g) all-purpose flour

3 oz (85 g) blueberries, washed and dried

1 tbsp (15 ml) lemon juice

FOR THE TOPPING

⅔ cup (151 g) light brown sugar

⅓ cup (62 g) all-purpose flour

⅓ cup (27 g) quick oats

6 tbsp (86 g) unsalted butter, cold

3 oz (85 g) blueberries, washed and dried (optional)

FOR THE CRUST

Prepare a 9 × 3-inch (23 × 8-cm) springform pan by lightly greasing the edges of the pan with cooking spray, and then wiping gently with a paper towel. Before measuring, grind the graham crackers into fine crumbs using a food processor or blender. In a medium-size bowl, combine the graham cracker crumbs and the brown sugar. Microwave the butter for 45 to 60 seconds until the butter is melted. Stir the melted butter into the crumbs until there are no dry crumbs left. Pour the crumbs into your springform pan and press firmly into the bottom and up the sides to create a thick crust.

FOR THE CHEESECAKE

Prepare the whipped cream first by placing the mixing bowl and whisk attachment in the freezer for 5 to 10 minutes to chill. Pour the heavy whipping cream into the chilled bowl and use an electric mixer to beat the heavy cream on medium-high speed until the cream gets bubbly. Slowly add the powdered sugar and continue beating on high speed until stiff peaks form. Set aside.

Melt the white chocolate in a microwave-safe bowl in 30-second increments, stirring each time until the chocolate is melted and smooth. I suggest microwaving at 50 percent power, which helps prevent the white chocolate from seizing. Allow the chocolate to cool.

Beat the cream cheese on medium-high speed for 2 to 3 minutes until it's light and fluffy. Add ½ cup (96 g) of sugar and the flour, and beat just until incorporated. Next, pour the melted white chocolate into the cream cheese mixture and blend until well incorporated. Scrape down the sides of the bowl.

Combine the blueberries, lemon juice and the remaining 1 tablespoon (12 g) of sugar in a food processor. Blend together until it reaches a liquid consistency. Next, pour the blueberry juice into the cream cheese mixture and beat on low speed until it is blended into the filling, scraping down the bowl as needed. Slowly add the prepared whipped cream into the cream cheese mixture, folding over and over with a spatula until the whipped cream is well combined. Pour the filling into the prepared crust and use a spatula to spread it evenly.

(continued)

blueberry crumble
CHEESECAKE (CONT.)

FOR THE TOPPING

Combine all of the dry ingredients in a medium-size bowl. Cut the butter into small cubes and add it to the dry ingredients. Use a pastry cutter or 2 forks to press the cold butter into the dry ingredients repeatedly until there are no loose and dry ingredients. Don't be afraid to use your (clean) hands! The mixture will be clumpy like dough. Break the dough apart and sprinkle it over the top of the cheesecake filling, and then gently press the crumbs down so they hold together.

Cover and refrigerate for at least 4 hours. If needed, gently run a warm knife around the top edge of the cheesecake to separate it from the sides of the pan. Garnish with fresh blueberries, if desired. To get nice crisp cuts, I freeze the cake for 30 minutes prior to serving. To serve, cut into this cake with a sharp knife, and clean the knife after each cut.

brownie batter CHEESECAKE

Do you ever get the hankering for a late night brownie? I know I do. Sometimes I want to make a batch of brownies just so I can lick the bowl! During the creation of my Brownie Batter Cheesecake, no actual brownies were harmed. I did, however, make batch after batch of this cheesecake until I got the brownie filling just right. The filling is flavored with a dry brownie mix batter, but the glaze is really where it's at! Put on your stretchy pants for this one, I am sure you won't be able to stop after one slice.

YIELD: 8 TO 10 SLICES

FOR THE CRUST

2 ½ cups (225 g) chocolate sandwich cookie crumbs (I use Oreos)

6 tbsp (86 g) unsalted butter

FOR THE FILLING

24 oz (680 g) cream cheese, softened

½ cup (96 g) granulated sugar

3 tbsp (44 ml) heavy whipping cream

2 tsp (10 ml) vanilla extract

3 cups (375 g) brownie mix (dry)

FOR THE GLAZE

3 tbsp (23 g) brownie mix (dry)

3 tsp (15 ml) vegetable oil

4 tbsp (59 ml) heavy whipping cream (or milk)

FOR THE TOPPING

1 cup (237 ml) heavy whipping cream

½ cup (65 g) powdered sugar

FOR THE CRUST

Prepare a 9-inch (23-cm) springform pan by lightly greasing the edges of the pan with cooking spray, and then wiping gently with a paper towel. Before measuring, grind the cookies into fine crumbs using a food processor or blender. In a microwave-safe bowl, microwave the butter for 45 to 60 seconds until the butter is melted. In a separate medium-size bowl, pour the melted butter into the cookie crumbs and stir until there are no dry crumbs left. Pour the crumbs into your springform pan and press firmly into the bottom and up the sides of your springform pan to create a thick crust.

FOR THE FILLING

Beat the cream cheese on medium-high speed for 2 to 3 minutes until it's light and fluffy. Slowly add the sugar into the cream cheese while beating the mixture. Next, add the heavy whipping cream and vanilla extract. Beat until the filling is smooth and creamy, scraping down the bowl as needed. Slowly add the dry brownie mix, beating on medium speed until the dry mix is completely blended into the cream cheese. Pour the filling into the prepared crust and spread evenly. Cover and refrigerate for 4 hours until the filling is firm.

FOR THE GLAZE

In a small bowl, combine dry brownie mix, vegetable oil and heavy whipping cream or milk. Whisk until the mixture is smooth. For a thinner mixture, you can add additional heavy whipping cream. Drizzle over the cheesecake.

FOR THE TOPPING

Place the mixing bowl and whisk attachment in the freezer for 5 to 10 minutes to chill. Pour the heavy whipping cream into the chilled bowl and use an electric mixer to beat the heavy cream on medium-high speed until the cream gets bubbly. Slowly add the powdered sugar and continue beating on high speed until stiff peaks form. Remove the springform pan edge and use a large star tip to pipe the whipped cream on the outside edges of the cheesecake.

chocolate cookie dough
CHEESECAKE

For a cookie dough cheescake, it's only fitting that it be loaded with lots of chocolate and stuffed with cookie dough.
It's filled with 3 types of chocolate: chocolate chips, cocoa powder and hot fudge sauce. This is the type of dessert you
see in the pastry case that makes your heart flutter. It is the ultimate indulgence. You won't be sorry. I'm certainly not.

YIELD: 8 TO 10 SLICES

FOR THE COOKIE DOUGH

8 tbsp (115 g) unsalted butter

½ cup (96 g) granulated sugar

⅓ cup (73 g) light brown sugar

1 ¼ cups (156 g) all-purpose flour

¼ tsp salt

2 tsp (10 ml) vanilla extract

½ cup (90 g) mini–chocolate chips

FOR THE CRUST

1 (13-oz [368-g]) package chocolate chip cookies (Chips Ahoy or similar brand)

¼ cup (55 g) light brown sugar

¼ cup (31 g) all-purpose flour

8 tbsp (115 g) unsalted butter

FOR THE FILLING

5 oz (142 g) dark chocolate chips

1 cup plus 2 tbsp (266 ml) heavy whipping cream, divided

½ cup (65 g) powdered sugar

16 oz (454 g) cream cheese, softened

¼ cup (48 g) granulated sugar

2 tbsp (14 g) unsweetened cocoa powder

¼ cup (59 ml) hot fudge sauce

FOR THE TOPPING

¾ cup (177 ml) heavy whipping cream

½ cup (65 g) powdered sugar

2 tbsp (30 ml) hot fudge sauce

FOR THE COOKIE DOUGH

Start by softening the butter in the microwave for 15 seconds. In a medium-size bowl, mix the softened butter with the sugar and brown sugar, and beat until it's light and fluffy. Add the flour, salt and vanilla extract, and mix until dough forms. Lastly, mix in the chocolate chips. Remove the dough from the bowl and make tiny cookie dough balls about the size of a dime. Set aside.

FOR THE CRUST

Prepare a 9-inch (23-cm) springform pan by lightly greasing the edges of the pan with cooking spray, and then wiping gently with a paper towel. Grind the cookies into fine crumbs using a food processor or blender. In a large bowl, combine the cookie crumbs, brown sugar and flour. In a microwave-safe bowl, microwave the butter for 45 to 60 seconds until the butter is melted. In a separate medium-size bowl, pour the melted butter over the cookie crumbs and stir until there are no dry crumbs left. Pour the crumbs into your springform pan and press firmly into the bottom and up the sides to create a thick crust.

FOR THE FILLING

In a microwave-safe bowl, combine the dark chocolate chips and 2 tablespoons (30 ml) of heavy whipping cream. Microwave for 30 to 60 seconds until the chocolate starts to melt. Remove it from the microwave and whisk the chocolate until it's smooth. Set aside.

Prepare the whipped cream by chilling your mixing bowl and whisk attachment in the freezer for 5 to 10 minutes. Pour the remaining 1 cup (237 ml) of heavy whipping cream into the chilled bowl and use an electric mixer to beat the heavy cream on medium-high speed until the cream gets bubbly. Slowly add the powdered sugar and continue beating on high speed until stiff peaks form. Set aside.

(continued)

chocolate cookie dough
CHEESECAKE (CONT.)

In a medium-size bowl, beat the cream cheese on medium-high speed for 2 to 3 minutes until it's light and fluffy. Add the granulated sugar and beat until it's well mixed. Next, pour the melted dark chocolate into the cream cheese and blend until well incorporated. Lastly, add the cocoa powder and the hot fudge sauce, and mix until the batter is completely smooth, scraping down the bowl as needed.

Slowly add the prepared whipped cream into the cream cheese mixture, folding over and over with a spatula until the whipped cream is well combined. Next, mix about ⅔ of the cookie dough balls into the filling with a spatula. Pour the filling into the prepared crust and smooth the top with a spatula. Cover and refrigerate for at least 4 hours until the filling is firm.

FOR THE TOPPING

Combine the whipping cream and powdered sugar, as described above, to prepare a second batch of whipped cream. Remove the springform pan edge and use a large star tip to pipe a boarder on the outside edges of the cheesecake.

Slice the remaining cookie dough pieces in half and place them over the top of the cheesecake before serving. Heat the hot fudge sauce in the microwave for 30 seconds. Drizzle the hot sauce over the top of the cookie dough. To get a nice clean slice when serving, wipe off the knife between cuts.

champagne cranberry
CHEESECAKE

If you meet me for brunch, I'll probably have a mimosa in hand. I just love the combination of champagne with a splash of orange juice! The first time I made this mimosa-inspired cheesecake, I took one bite and knew it was going to be a hit. The tangy cheesecake filling is spiked with champagne, zested with orange peel and swirled with white chocolate. It's quite the elegant dessert.

If you don't want to purchase an entire bottle of champagne, I like to get the single-serving mini bottles, because one bottle is all you need for this cheesecake. This dessert is garnished with sugared cranberries, which makes it just gorgeous. The one thing you need to keep in mind is the sugared cranberries need to sit overnight, so plan accordingly. You don't need a special occasion to celebrate with this cheesecake.

YIELD: 8 TO 10 SLICES

FOR THE CRANBERRIES
¾ cup (177 ml) water

1 ¾ cups (335 g) granulated sugar, divided

1 cup (99 g) cranberries, fresh

FOR THE CRUST
2 cups (180 g) graham cracker crumbs

6 tbsp (86 g) unsalted butter

FOR THE CHEESECAKE
10 oz (284 g) white chocolate chips

1 ¼ cups plus 5 tbsp (370 ml) heavy whipping cream, divided

1 cup (130 g) powdered sugar

16 oz (454 g) cream cheese, softened

⅓ cup (79 ml) champagne

Zest of 1 large orange

FOR THE CRANBERRIES
In a small saucepan, combine the water and ¾ cup (144 g) sugar and bring to a simmer, whisking the sugar until it dissolves. Remove the mixture from the heat and allow it to cool for 15 minutes. Add the cranberries to the sugar water, then cover and refrigerate overnight, stirring the cranberries occasionally to coat them. Line a rimmed baking sheet with parchment or wax paper, and place a wire rack on top of it. Using a slotted spoon, scoop the cranberries out of the syrup and drip off the excess syrup. Place the cranberries on the wire rack. Sprinkle ½ cup (96 g) of sugar over the cranberries and let sit for 10 minutes. Gently roll the cranberries over and sprinkle another ½ cup (96 g) of sugar on the other side. Once the cranberries are lightly coated in sugar on all sides, spoon them into a bowl and roll them in the remaining sugar that dripped off the cranberries into the sheet pan. Place the cranberries back on the wire rack to dry for about 1 hour.

FOR THE CRUST
Prepare a 9-inch (23-cm) springform pan by lightly greasing the edges of the pan with cooking spray, and then wiping gently with a paper towel. Before measuring, grind the graham crackers into fine crumbs using a food processor or blender. In a microwave-safe bowl, microwave the butter for 45 to 60 seconds until the butter is melted. In a separate medium-size bowl, pour the melted butter into the graham cracker crumbs and stir until there are no dry crumbs left. Pour the crumbs into your springform pan and press firmly into the bottom of the pan to form a thick crust. Set aside.

(continued)

champagne cranberry
CHEESECAKE (CONT.)

FOR THE CHEESECAKE

In a microwave-safe bowl, combine the white chocolate with 5 tablespoons (74 ml) of heavy whipping cream and microwave in 30-second increments, stirring each time until the chocolate is melted and smooth. I suggest microwaving at 50 percent power, which helps prevent the white chocolate from seizing. Allow the chocolate to cool.

Chill your mixing bowl and whisk attachment in the freezer for 5 to 10 minutes. Pour the remaining 1 ¼ cups (296 ml) of heavy whipping cream into the chilled bowl and use an electric mixer to beat the heavy cream on medium-high speed until the cream gets bubbly. Slowly add the powdered sugar and continue beating on high speed until stiff peaks form. Set the whipped cream aside.

Beat the cream cheese on medium-high speed for 2 to 3 minutes until it's light and fluffy. Next, pour the cooled white chocolate mixture into the cream cheese and blend until well incorporated, scraping down the bowl as needed. Slowly pour the champagne into the cream cheese while continuing to beat the mixture. Next, add the orange zest and mix until incorporated. Slowly add the prepared whipped cream into the cream cheese mixture, folding over and over with a spatula until the whipped cream is well combined. Pour the filling into the prepared crust. Cover with foil and refrigerate for 4 hours.

I like to add the sugared cranberries right before serving. The sugar coating will eventually come off if it sits for too long on the surface of the cheesecake.

piña colada CHEESECAKE

This was one of the first desserts I made for this cookbook. I knew I wanted a piña colada cheesecake, but it had to be just right. This dessert features a thick, buttery vanilla crust with a dense shredded coconut cheesecake filling spiked with rum. Once you take a bite with the fresh pineapple and the creamy cheesecake, you won't stop until you have finished the whole slice!

I have garnished this cheesecake with maraschino cherries, which are usually very juicy. I prefer to allow the cherries to sit on a paper towel (the longer the better) before I add them to the cheesecake. Otherwise, the juice from the cherries will run down the sides of the whipped cream. It's up to you, though; maybe that is the look you are going for! You can use canned pineapples for this recipe, but be sure they are well drained before adding them to the cheesecake; I prefer fresh pineapple myself.

YIELD: 8 TO 10 SLICES

FOR THE CRUST

11 oz (312 g) vanilla wafers (I use Nilla wafers)

8 tbsp (115 g) unsalted butter

FOR THE CHEESECAKE

24 oz (680 g) cream cheese, softened

½ cup (96 g) granulated sugar

3 tbsp (44 ml) heavy whipping cream

1 tbsp (15 ml) spiced rum, or 1 tsp imitation rum extract to avoid using alcohol (optional)

½ tsp coconut extract

2 cups (152 g) shredded coconut

FOR THE TOPPING

1 cup (237 ml) heavy whipping cream

½ cup (65 g) powdered sugar

1 ½ cups (270 g) diced pineapple

14 to 16 Maraschino cherries for garnish (optional)

FOR THE CRUST

Prepare a 9-inch (23-cm) springform pan by lightly greasing the edges of the pan with cooking spray, and then wiping gently with a paper towel. Grind the wafers into fine crumbs using a food processor or blender. In a microwave-safe bowl, microwave the butter for 45 to 60 seconds until the butter is melted. In a separate medium-size bowl, pour the melted butter into the crumbs and stir until there are no dry crumbs left. Pour the crumbs into your springform pan and press firmly into the bottom and up the sides to create a thick crust. Refrigerate the crust until the filling is ready.

FOR THE CHEESECAKE

Beat the cream cheese on medium-high speed for 2 to 3 minutes until it's light and fluffy. Slowly add the sugar into the cream cheese while beating the mixture. Next, add the heavy whipping cream, spiced rum and coconut extract. To make a nonalcoholic version, consider using 1 teaspoon of rum extract instead of the spiced rum. Start with your mixer on a low speed to incorporate the liquid into the cream cheese mixture, and then increase the speed to medium-high. Beat on medium-high for another 2 minutes, scraping down the bowl as needed. Lastly, add the shredded coconut and mix it into the cream cheese until well blended. Pour the filling into the prepared crust. Cover with foil and refrigerate for 4 hours.

FOR THE TOPPING

Chill your mixing bowl and whisk attachment in the freezer for 5 to 10 minutes. Pour the heavy whipping cream into the chilled bowl and use an electric mixer to beat the heavy cream on medium-high speed until the cream gets bubbly. Slowly add the powdered sugar and continue beating on high speed until stiff peaks form. Remove the springform pan edge and use a large star tip to pipe the whipped cream on the outside edges of the cheesecake. Garnish with fresh pineapple when ready to serve. You can also top with cherries, if desired.

iced animal
COOKIE CHEESECAKE

There is so much to love with this Iced Animal Cookie Cheesecake. Not only it is loaded with sprinkles, but there are plenty of iced animal cookies both in the crust and the cheesecake filling. Let's be honest, it's hard to resist breaking into a bag of iced animal cookies. They're coated in pink or white chocolate and garnished with sprinkles. To make this cheesecake a little extra special, I've added a bit of dry vanilla cake mix which adds some cake batter flavor.

YIELD: 10 TO 12 SLICES

FOR THE CRUST

1 cup (90 g) iced animal cookie crumbs

1 ½ cups (135 g) vanilla sandwich cookie crumbs (I use Golden Oreos)

4 tbsp (57 g) unsalted butter

FOR THE FILLING

1 cup plus 2 tbsp (267 ml) heavy whipping cream, divided

½ cup (65 g) powdered sugar

16 oz (454 g) cream cheese, softened

2 tsp (10 ml) vanilla extract

¼ cup (48 g) granulated sugar

½ cup (65 g) dry vanilla cake mix

2 cups (180 g) crushed iced animal cookies

FOR THE TOPPING

¾ cup (177 ml) heavy whipping cream

½ cup (65 g) powdered sugar

¼ cup (57 g) sprinkles

FOR THE CRUST

Prepare a 9-inch (23-cm) springform pan by lightly greasing the edges of the pan with cooking spray, and then wiping gently with a paper towel. Before measuring, grind the iced animal cookies into fine crumbs using a food processor or blender. Repeat this step with the vanilla sandwich cookies and then mix the crumbs together. In a microwave-safe bowl, microwave the butter for 45 to 60 seconds until the butter is melted. In a separate medium-size bowl, pour the melted butter into the crumbs and stir until there are no dry crumbs left. Pour the crumbs into your springform pan and press firmly into the bottom of the pan to form the crust.

FOR THE FILLING

Prepare the whipped cream first by placing the mixing bowl and whisk attachment in the freezer for 5 to 10 minutes to chill. Pour 1 cup (237 ml) of heavy whipping cream into the chilled bowl and use an electric mixer to beat the heavy cream on medium-high speed until the cream gets bubbly. Slowly add the powdered sugar and continue beating on high speed until stiff peaks form. Set aside.

In a separate bowl, beat the cream cheese on medium-high speed for 2 to 3 minutes until it's light and fluffy. Add the vanilla extract and remaining 2 tablespoons (30 ml) of heavy whipping cream and beat until incorporated. Next, add the granulated sugar and dry vanilla cake mix, and beat until well incorporated, scraping down the bowl as needed.

Place the iced animal cookies in a large plastic bag, such as a Ziploc bag, and smash them into pieces with a heavy kitchen tool such as a rolling pin. You want a good mix of crumbs and small chunks. Add 2 cups (180 g) of the crushed cookies to the cream cheese mixture and mix until combined. Then add the prepared whipped cream to the cream cheese mixture and mix until all of the ingredients are well combined to form your cheesecake filling. Pour the filling into the prepared crust. Cover and refrigerate for 4 to 6 hours.

FOR THE TOPPING

Prepare a second batch of whipped cream for piping as described above using heavy whipping cream and powdered sugar. Before removing from the springform pan, pour the sprinkles over the top of the cheesecake and gently shake the pan back and forth to evenly coat the top, gently pressing into the cheesecake if needed. Remove the springform pan edge and pipe the whipped cream along the border of the cheesecake.

red velvet CHEESECAKE

I know more than a few of you reading this love red velvet. I couldn't leave you hanging. What really makes a red velvet dessert is the subtle chocolate flavor achieved by adding cocoa powder to an otherwise vanilla dessert. My Red Velvet Cheesecake has an added layer of chocolate truffle ganache and some fresh whipped cream on top. Every bite is filled with plenty of chocolate and that classic cheesecake flavor you are craving.

YIELD: 8 TO 10 SLICES

FOR THE CRUST

1 (14-oz [405-g]) package chocolate sandwich cookie (I use Oreos)

8 tbsp (115 g) unsalted butter

FOR THE CHEESECAKE

1 cup plus 2 tbsp (266 ml) heavy whipping cream, divided

½ cup (65 g) powdered sugar

4 oz (113 g) white chocolate chips

12 oz (340 g) cream cheese, softened

½ cup (96 g) granulated sugar

2 tbsp (14 g) cocoa powder

1 tbsp (15 ml) red food coloring gel

FOR THE TOPPING

6 oz (170 g) dark chocolate chips

2 cups (473 ml) heavy whipping cream, divided

¾ cup (98 g) powdered sugar

¼ cup (45 g) mini–chocolate chips

FOR THE CRUST

Prepare a 9-inch (23-cm) springform pan by lightly greasing the edges of the pan with cooking spray, and then wiping gently with a paper towel. Grind the cookies into fine crumbs using a food processor or blender. In a microwave-safe bowl, microwave the butter for 45 to 60 seconds until the butter is melted. In a separate medium-size bowl, pour the melted butter into the cookie crumbs and stir until there are no dry crumbs left. Pour the crumbs into your springform pan and press firmly into the bottom and up the sides of the pan to form a thick crust.

FOR THE CHEESECAKE

To prepare the whipped cream, place the mixing bowl and whisk attachment in the freezer for 5 to 10 minutes to chill. Pour 1 cup (237 ml) of heavy whipping cream into the chilled bowl and use an electric mixer to beat the heavy cream on medium-high speed until the cream gets bubbly. Slowly add the powdered sugar and continue beating on high speed until stiff peaks form. Set the whipped cream aside.

In a microwave-safe bowl, combine white chocolate chips with remaining 2 tablespoons (30 ml) of heavy whipping cream and microwave in 30-second increments, stirring each time until the chocolate is melted and smooth. I suggest microwaving at 50 percent power, which helps prevent the white chocolate from seizing. Allow the chocolate mixture to cool.

Beat the cream cheese on medium-high speed for 2 to 3 minutes until it's light and fluffy. Add the granulated sugar and cocoa powder and beat at a low speed until incorporated. Increase the speed to medium-high and beat until well combined, scraping down the sides of the bowl as needed. Add the white chocolate and beat on medium-high speed until well mixed. Lastly, add the red food coloring a little at a time until the desired batter color is reached. Keep in mind that after adding the whipped cream, the batter will be much lighter in color. Slowly add the prepared whipped cream into the cream cheese mixture, folding over and over with a spatula until the whipped cream is well combined. Pour the filling into the prepared crust. Cover with foil and refrigerate for 4 hours.

(continued)

red velvet CHEESECAKE (CONT.)

FOR THE TOPPING

In a microwave-safe bowl, combine dark chocolate chips with ½ cup (118 ml) of heavy whipping cream. Microwave for 60 seconds and then stir until the chocolate is completely smooth. Spread the chocolate ganache over the top of the cheesecake using a spatula to push it to the edges.

Prepare a second batch of whipped cream as described above using the remaining 1 ½ cups (355 ml) of heavy whipping cream and ¾ cup (98 g) of powdered sugar. Remove the springform pan edge and pipe the whipped cream in a large zigzag pattern or simply spread evenly over the top of the cheesecake. Sprinkle the whipped cream with mini–chocolate chips. Keep the cheesecake covered in the refrigerator.

(tip from julianne) No one likes red velvet to taste like dye. So instead of using traditional food coloring, I buy the gels. These are thicker, allowing you to use less to achieve the red color. Gels can be purchased at most craft stores. You can also buy a "no taste" red, which helps when you need a lot of red dye and don't want all of the dye flavor.

peppermint oreo
CHOCOLATE CHEESECAKE

Everyone needs a home run dessert to serve during the holidays. I love peppermint and it's game on as soon as Thanksgiving is over. This cheesecake is layers of fun. It starts with an Oreo cookie crust and it's filled with an Oreo peppermint cheesecake. In the cheesecake, you'll find not only crushed cookies but also chopped peppermint white chocolate. Then, you have a layer of homemade, thick chocolate pudding and finally it's topped with a layer of fresh whipped cream. There is a lot of love about this cheesecake, and all those glorious layers. Be sure to read through all of the steps before you begin, as there is a waiting period between steps. This dessert takes a bit longer to prepare, but trust me when I say, "it's worth the wait!"

YIELD: 8 TO 10 SLICES

FOR THE PUDDING

2 large egg yolks, slightly beaten

2 tbsp (16 g) all-purpose flour

⅓ cup (64 g) granulated sugar

Dash of salt

1 cup (237 ml) milk

½ tsp vanilla extract

6 oz (170 g) dark chocolate chips

FOR THE CRUST

2 cups (180 g) Oreo crumbs (or similar chocolate sandwich cookie)

5 tbsp (72 g) unsalted butter

FOR THE CHEESECAKE

16 oz (454 g) cream cheese, softened

2 tbsp (30 ml) heavy whipping cream

⅓ cup (64 g) granulated sugar

1 cup (180 g) finely chopped peppermint white chocolate

½ tsp peppermint extract

10 Oreo cookies (or similar chocolate sandwich cookie), crushed

FOR THE TOPPING

1 ½ cups (355 ml) heavy whipping cream

¾ cup (98 g) powdered sugar

2 tbsp (44 g) hot fudge sauce

FOR THE PUDDING

Measure out all of the ingredients for the pudding prior to starting. Place the egg yolks in a separate bowl. In a medium-size saucepan, add the flour, sugar and salt, and whisk to combine. Add the milk and vanilla extract. Heat the mixture on the stove top over medium-low heat. Whisk constantly to dissolve the dry ingredients into the milk mixture. Once the mixture is warm (but not boiling), pour about ¼ cup (59 ml) of it into the bowl with the egg yolks and whisk vigorously to temper the egg yolks. Immediately pour the egg yolks into the saucepan and continue whisking over medium-low heat to prevent the eggs from cooking. Whisk until the pudding starts to thicken. Add the chocolate chips to the mixture and continue whisking over medium-low heat until the chocolate melts and the pudding starts to thicken. It will happen very quickly.

Strain the pudding through a fine sieve into a medium-size bowl. This step is optional, but it will help catch any lumps of ingredients that did not get blended. Immediately cover the top of the pudding with clear plastic wrap (directly on the surface of the pudding) and poke a few holes with a toothpick. Allow it to cool on the counter for at least 1 hour before refrigerating. Refrigerate for 2 to 3 hours until the pudding has cooled and is firm.

FOR THE CRUST

Prepare a 9-inch (23-cm) springform pan by lightly greasing the edges of the pan with cooking spray, and then wiping gently with a paper towel. Before measuring, grind the cookies into fine crumbs using a food processor or blender. In a microwave-safe bowl, microwave the butter for 45 to 60 seconds until the butter is melted. In a separate medium-size bowl, pour the melted butter into the cookie crumbs and stir until there are no dry crumbs left. Pour the crumbs into your springform pan and press firmly into the bottom to form a thick crust. Set aside.

(continued)

peppermint oreo
CHOCOLATE CHEESECAKE (CONT.)

FOR THE CHEESECAKE

Using a medium-size bowl, beat the cream cheese and heavy whipping cream on medium-high speed for 3 to 4 minutes until it's light and fluffy, and scrape down the sides of the bowl as needed. Add the sugar and continue beating for 2 to 3 minutes until well incorporated. Next, add the chopped white chocolate and peppermint extract, and mix until well combined. Lastly, add the crushed Oreos and fold into the cream cheese with a spatula until well combined. Pour the cheesecake filling into the prepared crust. Then, spread your cooled chocolate pudding over the cheesecake filling, smoothing with a spatula.

FOR THE TOPPING

Chill your mixing bowl and whisk attachment in the freezer for 5 to 10 minutes. Pour the heavy whipping cream into the chilled bowl and use an electric mixer to beat the heavy cream on medium-high speed until the cream gets bubbly. Slowly add the powdered sugar and continue beating on high speed until stiff peaks form.

Set aside 1 cup (60 g) of whipped cream for piped edges. Spread the remaining whipped cream over the top of the pudding. Use a large star tip to pipe the whipped cream on the outside edges of the cheesecake. Lastly, heat the hot fudge sauce according to the instructions on the jar and drizzle it over the whipped cream. The cheesecake must be refrigerated for at least 4 hours before serving to allow the layers to set properly.

apple pie CHEESECAKE

My cheesecake chapter wouldn't be complete without my Apple Pie Cheesecake. I love making apple pie filling on the stove top, it is way easier than you think and can be used for a variety of desserts. The apple pie filling complements the brown sugar cheesecake with a graham cracker crust. The autumn season is my favorite time of year, and that is when I miss Vermont the most. Activities such as apple picking are high on my priority list for when I visit in the fall. However, you don't need to wait for the autumn season to enjoy this apple dessert; it's good all year round! In my apple filling, I usually like to use green apples, but feel free to use your favorite type of apple.

YIELD: 8 TO 10 SLICES

FOR THE FILLING

3 medium green apples

2 tsp (10 ml) fresh lemon juice

1 tbsp (15 ml) maple syrup

2 tbsp (12 g) all-purpose flour

2 tsp (5 g) cinnamon

2 tbsp (29 g) unsalted butter

FOR THE CRUST

2 ¼ cups (202 g) graham cracker crumbs

¼ cup (55 g) light brown sugar

2 tsp (5 g) cinnamon

8 tbsp (115 g) unsalted butter

FOR THE CHEESECAKE

16 oz (454 g) cream cheese, softened

⅓ cup (67 g) light brown sugar

2 tbsp (30 ml) heavy whipping cream

1 tsp cinnamon

FOR THE TOPPING

¾ cup (177 ml) heavy whipping cream

½ cup (65 g) powdered sugar

Cinnamon for garnish as desired

FOR THE FILLING

Peel and dice the apples (about the size of a dime) into your saucepan. Squeeze the fresh lemon juice over the top of the apples. Next, add the maple syrup, flour, cinnamon and butter into the saucepan and stir to combine all of the ingredients. Cook the apple filling over medium-low heat, stirring occasionally for 12 to 15 minutes until the apples are softened and the filling thickens. Remove the apple filling from the heat and allow it to cool completely.

FOR THE CRUST

Prepare a 9-inch (23-cm) springform pan by lightly greasing the edges of the pan with cooking spray, and then wiping gently with a paper towel. Before measuring, grind the graham crackers into fine crumbs using a food processor or blender. Combine it with the brown sugar and the cinnamon in a medium-size bowl. In a microwave-safe bowl, microwave the butter for 45 to 60 seconds until the butter is melted. Pour the melted butter into the graham cracker crumbs and stir until there are no dry crumbs left. Pour the crumbs into your springform pan and press firmly into the bottom and up the sides of the pan to create a thick crust.

FOR THE CHEESECAKE

Beat the softened cream cheese on medium-high speed for 2 to 3 minutes until it's light and fluffy. Slowly add the brown sugar into the cream cheese while beating the mixture. Next, add the heavy whipping cream and cinnamon, and beat until the filling is smooth and creamy, scraping the bowl as needed. Pour the filling into the prepared crust and refrigerate for 2 hours. After refrigerating, spread the cooled apple filling over the cheesecake.

FOR THE TOPPING

Place the mixing bowl and whisk attachment in the freezer for 5 to 10 minutes to chill. Pour the heavy whipping cream into the chilled bowl and use an electric mixer to beat the heavy cream on medium-high speed until the cream gets bubbly. Slowly add the powdered sugar and continue beating on high speed until stiff peaks form. Remove the springform pan edge and use a large star tip to pipe the whipped cream on the border of the cheesecake and sprinkle cinnamon on top.

(two)

no-bake pies

A slice of pie is all you need to brighten your day. In this chapter you'll find sky-high pies such as my Mexican Chocolate Mousse Pie (page 54) as well as mash-ups like my Hot Mess Nutella Snickers Pie (page 67). Perhaps you're looking for a boozy treat? Then you will want to try my Bourbon Butterscotch Pudding Pie (page 53). I love making my pies in a springform pan so I can remove the edges and easily slice the pie without losing all of the crust. However, some of these can be made in a traditional pie plate as well. A pile of whipped cream and a lot of crust are two requirements for my pies.

bourbon butterscotch
PUDDING PIE

This pie is inspired by a dessert I had during my first trip to Seattle. I had never thought to make a butterscotch pie before. However, after tasting that pie in Seattle, I knew a butterscotch pie would be a great addition to my book. The key to making a great butterscotch pudding is adding brown sugar and melted butter. This pie is spiked with a subtle touch of bourbon, which is such a nice complement to the butterscotch flavor. If you want to make this without alcohol, simply omit it from both the filling and the whipped topping. Don't be intimidated by the homemade pudding; it really is quite simple.

YIELD: 8 SLICES

FOR THE CRUST

2 ¼ cups (202 g) graham cracker crumbs

8 tbsp (115 g) unsalted butter

FOR THE PUDDING

2 tbsp (29 g) unsalted butter

3 large egg yolks

¾ cup (151 g) light brown sugar

1 ½ cups (355 ml) milk

½ cup (118 ml) heavy whipping cream

3 tbsp (28 g) corn starch

1 tbsp (15 ml) bourbon

FOR THE TOPPING

¾ cup (177 ml) heavy whipping cream

2 tsp (10 ml) bourbon

½ cup (65 g) powdered sugar

¼ cup (30 g) pecans, crushed

FOR THE CRUST

Prepare a 9-inch (23-cm) springform pan by lightly greasing the edges of the pan with cooking spray, and then wiping gently with a paper towel. Before measuring, grind the graham crackers into fine crumbs using a food processor or blender. In a microwave-safe bowl, microwave the butter for 45 to 60 seconds until the butter is melted. In a separate medium-size bowl, pour the melted butter into the graham cracker crumbs and stir until there are no dry crumbs left. Pour the crumbs into your springform pan and press firmly into the bottom and up on the sides to create a thick crust.

FOR THE PUDDING

Measure out all of the ingredients for the pudding prior to starting. You will need to work quickly to prevent the eggs from becoming scrambled. In a medium-size saucepan, melt the butter over medium-low heat. Once the butter is melted, add the egg yolks, whisking continuously until well combined. Immediately add the brown sugar and whisk into the eggs. Quickly add the milk and heavy whipping cream, continuing to whisk over medium-low heat. Add the cornstarch 1 tablespoon (9 g) at a time, and whisk until dissolved. Once the pudding starts to thicken, continue cooking for another couple of minutes until it is bubbling lightly.

Remove the pudding from the heat and whisk in the bourbon (if desired), stirring rapidly until the pudding is well blended. Strain the pudding through a fine sieve into the prepared crust. This step is optional, but it will help catch any lumps of ingredients that did not get blended. Immediately cover the top of the pudding with clear plastic wrap (directly on the surface of the pudding) and poke a few holes with a toothpick. Allow it to cool on the counter for at least 1 hour before refrigerating. Refrigerate the pie for 4 to 6 hours until the filling is firm before adding the topping.

FOR THE TOPPING

Place the mixing bowl and whisk attachment in the freezer for 5 to 10 minutes to chill. Pour the heavy whipping cream and bourbon (if desired) into the chilled bowl and use an electric mixer to beat the heavy cream on medium-high speed until the cream gets bubbly. Slowly add the powdered sugar and continue beating on high speed until stiff peaks form. Spread the whipped cream over the top of the pie and garnish with crushed pecans.

mexican chocolate
MOUSSE PIE

I don't normally add spices to chocolate, but this pie has changed everything. When I serve this pie to my friends and family, their first thought is, *whoa, that's a kick of flavor!* But they keep coming back for more. This one is for you, Jef!

YIELD: 8 TO 10 SLICES

FOR THE CRUST

1 (14-oz [405-g]) package chocolate sandwich cookies (I use Oreos)

8 tbsp (115 g) unsalted butter

FOR THE FILLING

2 tbsp (30 ml) hot water

1 tsp espresso powder

10 oz (284 g) dark chocolate chips

1 ½ cups plus 5 tbsp (429 ml) heavy whipping cream, divided

1 cup (130 g) powdered sugar

8 oz (227 g) cream cheese, softened

½ tsp cayenne pepper

1 tsp cinnamon

FOR THE TOPPING

1 cup (237 ml) heavy whipping cream

½ cup (65 g) powdered sugar

¼ tsp of cinnamon

FOR THE CRUST

Prepare a 9-inch (23-cm) springform pan by lightly greasing the edges of the pan with cooking spray, and then wiping gently with a paper towel. Grind the cookies into fine crumbs using a food processor or blender. In a microwave-safe bowl, microwave the butter for 45 to 60 seconds until the butter is melted. In a separate medium-size bowl, pour the melted butter into the cookie crumbs and stir until there are no dry crumbs left. Pour the crumbs into your springform pan and press firmly into the bottom and up on the sides to create a thick crust.

FOR THE FILLING

Place the mixing bowl and whisk attachment in the freezer for 5 to 10 minutes to chill. Prepare the next couple of steps while the bowl is freezing. Combine the hot water and the espresso powder in a small glass and whisk until the powder is dissolved. Set aside.

In a microwave-safe bowl, combine the dark chocolate chips and 5 tablespoons (74 ml) of heavy whipping cream. Microwave in 30-second increments, stirring occasionally until the chocolate starts to melt, then whisk until chocolate is completely smooth. Set aside to cool for 10 to 15 minutes.

To prepare the whipped cream, pour the remaining 1 ½ cups (355 ml) of heavy whipping cream into the chilled mixing bowl and use an electric mixer to beat the heavy cream on medium-high speed until the cream gets bubbly. Slowly add the powdered sugar and continue beating on high speed until stiff peaks form. Set the whipped cream aside.

Beat the cream cheese on medium-high speed for 2 to 3 minutes until it's light and fluffy, scraping down the sides of the bowl occasionally. Slowly add in the melted chocolate and beat on a low speed. Continue beating until the chocolate and the cream cheese are well combined, scraping down the bowl as needed. Measure out 3 teaspoons (15 ml) of the brewed espresso and add to the mousse along with the cayenne pepper and cinnamon. Beat the mousse until well incorporated. Lastly, add the prepared whipped cream and fold it into the mousse until the ingredients are well mixed. Pour the mousse filling into the prepared piecrust. Cover and refrigerate for 4 to 6 hours until the filling is firm. I prefer to add the whipped topping right before serving.

FOR THE TOPPING

Prepare the whipped cream for the topping as described above using the heavy whipping cream and powdered sugar. Use a large cookie scoop to add the whipped cream to the top of your pie, creating a two-tiered look. The bottom is usually 5 to 6 scoops and the top layer is 3 scoops. Sprinkle lightly with cinnamon on top.

dulce de leche PIE

My Dulce de Leche Pie is for very special occasions. The filling is light and airy and just melts in your mouth. Serve this pie with sliced strawberries and a big dollop of whipped cream. The pie has just the right amount of sweetness, which is balanced out by the white chocolate and cream cheese in the filling. Serve with a glass of champagne for a real treat!

YIELD: 8 TO 10 SLICES

FOR THE CRUST

1 (14-oz [405-g]) package chocolate sandwich cookies (I use Oreos)

8 tbsp (115 g) unsalted butter

FOR THE FILLING

10 oz (284 g) white chocolate

1 ¼ cups plus 5 tbsp (370 ml) heavy whipping cream, divided

1 cup (130 g) powdered sugar

8 oz (227 g) cream cheese, softened

¼ cup (59 ml) dulce de leche

FOR THE TOPPING

¾ cup (177 ml) heavy whipping cream

½ cup (65 g) powdered sugar

8 strawberries

FOR THE CRUST

Prepare a 9-inch (23-cm) springform pan by lightly greasing the edges of the pan with cooking spray, and then wiping gently with a paper towel. Grind the cookies into fine crumbs using a food processor or blender. In a microwave-safe bowl, microwave the butter for 45 to 60 seconds until the butter is melted. In a separate medium-size bowl, pour the melted butter into the cookie crumbs and stir until there are no dry crumbs left. Pour the crumbs into your springform pan and press firmly into the bottom and up the sides to create a thick crust.

FOR THE FILLING

Place the mixing bowl and whisk attachment in the freezer for 5 to 10 minutes to chill. Prepare the next step while the bowl is chilling.

In a microwave-safe bowl, combine the white chocolate and 5 tablespoons (74 ml) of heavy whipping cream. Microwave at 50 percent power for 60 to 90 seconds until the chocolate starts to melt, and then whisk vigorously until the chocolate is completely smooth. Set aside to cool for 10 to 15 minutes.

To prepare the whipped cream, pour the remaining 1 ¼ cups (296 ml) of heavy whipping cream into the chilled mixing bowl and use an electric mixer to beat the heavy cream on medium-high speed until the cream gets bubbly. Slowly add the powdered sugar and continue beating on high speed until stiff peaks form. Set aside.

Beat the cream cheese on medium-high speed for 2 to 3 minutes until it's light and fluffy, scraping down the sides of the bowl occasionally. Slowly pour in the melted white chocolate and beat on a low speed until the chocolate and cream cheese are well combined, scraping down the bowl as needed.

Microwave the dulce de leche for about 20 to 30 seconds until it can easily be stirred. Pour the dulce de leche into the cream cheese mixture and continue beating until all of the ingredients are well mixed to form your mousse. Lastly, fold the prepared whipped cream into the mousse until the mixture is well combined. Pour the mousse filling into the prepared piecrust and spread smoothly. Cover and refrigerate for 4 to 6 hours until the filling is firm.

FOR THE TOPPING

Prepare the whipped cream for the topping as described above using the heavy whipping cream and powdered sugar. Remove the springform pan edge and use a large star tip to pipe a border on the outside edges of the cheesecake. Slice the strawberries in half and place them on top of the whipped cream just before serving.

pumpkin MOUSSE PIE

I don't know about you, but in my opinion, pumpkin pie is acceptable all year round. For this pumpkin pie, I've added a few elements to make it extra special. You'll find a hint of white chocolate, a touch of cream cheese and some marshmallow crème. The marshmallow crème helps keep this pie extra light and fluffy. You will also see that this pie features a bit of dulce de leche both in the filling and drizzled on top. This is not to be missed! If you can't find the dulce de leche, I would suggest substituting with caramel sauce.

YIELD: 8 TO 10 SLICES

FOR THE CRUST

2 cups (180 g) graham cracker crumbs

2 tbsp (25 g) light brown sugar

1 tsp pumpkin pie spice

8 tbsp (115 g) unsalted butter

FOR THE FILLING

⅔ cup plus 2 tbsp (188 ml) heavy whipping cream, divided

⅓ cup (43 g) powdered sugar

4 oz (113 g) white chocolate chips

4 oz (113 g) cream cheese, softened

8 oz (226 g) pumpkin puree

½ tsp pumpkin pie spice

2 tbsp (44 g) dulce de leche

7 oz (198 g) marshmallow crème

FOR THE TOPPING

1 cup (237 ml) heavy whipping cream

½ cup (65 g) powdered sugar

2 tbsp (447 g) dulce de leche

FOR THE CRUST

Before measuring, grind the graham crackers into fine crumbs using a food processor or blender. In a medium-size bowl, combine the graham cracker crumbs, brown sugar and pumpkin pie spice. In a microwave-safe bowl, microwave the butter for 45 to 60 seconds until the butter is melted. Stir the butter into the crumbs until there are no dry crumbs left. If you want to be able to remove the tart from the bottom of the pan, cut a parchment circle the same size as the bottom of the pan. Pour the crumbs into a 9-inch (23-cm) tart pan and press firmly against the sides and bottom of the pan to form a thick crust.

FOR THE FILLING

Place the mixing bowl and whisk attachment in the freezer for 5 to 10 minutes to chill. Pour ⅔ cup (158 ml) of heavy whipping cream into the chilled bowl and use an electric mixer to beat the heavy cream on medium-high speed until the cream gets bubbly. Slowly add the powdered sugar and continue beating on high speed until stiff peaks form. Measure out 1 cup (75 g) of whipped cream for the filling. Any leftovers can be added to the topping.

In a microwave-safe bowl, melt the white chocolate chips together with remaining 2 tablespoons (30 ml) of heavy whipping cream in 20-second increments, stirring occasionally to prevent the chocolate from burning. I suggest microwaving at 50 percent power, which also helps prevent the white chocolate from seizing. Once melted, stir until it's smooth and set aside to cool.

In a medium-size bowl, beat the softened cream cheese on medium-high speed for 2 to 3 minutes until it's light and fluffy, and then scrape the sides of the bowl. Add the pumpkin puree and pumpkin pie spice and beat on medium speed until it's smooth, scraping down the bowl as needed. Next, add the melted white chocolate and dulce de leche and beat until incorporated. Lastly, add the jar of marshmallow crème and beat until all of the ingredients are well combined. Fold in the 1 cup (75 g) of the prepared whipped cream until incorporated. Pour the filling into the prepared crust. Cover and refrigerate for 1 hour.

FOR THE TOPPING

Combine the whipping cream and powdered sugar as described above to prepare a second batch of whipped cream. Spread the whipped cream over the top of the pumpkin pie and refrigerate it for at least 3 more hours until the filling has firmed up. Prior to serving, warm the dulce de leche in the microwave for 15 to 30 seconds and drizzle it over the whipped cream.

grasshopper PIE

When it comes to choosing a flavor of dessert, I am extremely partial to mint chocolate. There simply had to be a grasshopper pie in my cookbook. In my opinion, a grasshopper pie has to have a thick chocolate cookie crust, with a piled-high mint filling and more chocolate and whipped cream all over the top. I've decided to spice things up a bit and add a layer of chocolate pudding to balance out the mint filling. The filling has a light and airy texture, which is achieved by the addition of the marshmallow crème. Mint chocolate lovers will sure love this pie. Be sure to read through all of the steps before you begin, as there is a waiting period between steps.

YIELD: 8 TO 12 SLICES

FOR THE PUDDING

1 large egg yolk, slightly beaten

⅓ cup (64 g) granulated sugar

2 tbsp (16 g) all-purpose flour

Dash of salt

1 cup (237 ml) milk

½ tsp vanilla extract

6 oz (170 g) dark chocolate chips

FOR THE CRUST

2 ½ cups (225 g) chocolate sandwich cookie crumbs (I use Oreos)

6 tbsp (86 g) unsalted butter

FOR THE FILLING

1 ½ cups (355 ml) heavy whipping cream

¾ cup (98 g) powdered sugar

12 oz (340 g) cream cheese, softened

⅓ cup (64 g) granulated sugar

7 oz (198 g) marshmallow crème

¼ tsp mint extract

Green food coloring

1 ¼ cups (225 g) mini–chocolate chips

FOR THE TOPPING

1 ½ cups (355 ml) heavy whipping cream

¾ cup (98 g) powdered sugar

4 oz (113 g) chocolate bar (optional)

Hot fudge sauce

FOR THE PUDDING

Measure out all of the ingredients for the pudding prior to starting. Place the egg yolk in a separate bowl. In a medium-size saucepan, add the sugar, flour and salt, and whisk to combine. Add the milk and vanilla extract, and heat the mixture on the stove top over medium-low heat. Whisk constantly to dissolve the dry ingredients into the milk mixture. Once the milk is warm (but not boiling), pour about ¼ cup (59 ml) of it into the bowl with the egg yolk and whisk vigorously to temper the yolk. Immediately pour the egg yolk into the saucepan and continue whisking over medium-low heat to prevent the egg from cooking. Whisk until the pudding starts to thicken. Add the dark chocolate chips to the saucepan and whisk until completely melted. Remove it from the heat when the pudding starts to thicken.

Strain the pudding through a fine sieve into a medium-size bowl. This step is optional, but it will help catch any lumps of ingredients that did not get blended. Immediately cover the top of the pudding with clear plastic wrap (directly on the surface of the pudding) and poke a few holes with a toothpick. Allow the pudding to cool on the counter for at least 1 hour before refrigerating. Refrigerate for 2 to 3 hours until the pudding has cooled and is firm.

FOR THE CRUST

Prepare a 9-inch (23-cm) springform pan by lightly greasing the edges of the pan with cooking spray, and then wiping gently with a paper towel. Before measuring, grind the cookies into fine crumbs using a food processor or blender. In a microwave-safe bowl, microwave the butter for 45 to 60 seconds until the butter is melted. In a separate medium-size bowl, pour the melted butter into the cookie crumbs and stir until there are no dry crumbs left. Pour the crumbs into your springform pan and press firmly into the bottom and up the sides to create a thick crust.

(continued)

FOR THE FILLING

Place the mixing bowl and whisk attachment in the freezer for 5 to 10 minutes to chill. Pour the heavy whipping cream into the chilled bowl and use an electric mixer to beat the heavy cream on medium-high speed until the cream gets bubbly. Slowly add the powdered sugar and continue beating on high speed until stiff peaks form. Set the whipped cream aside.

Beat the cream cheese on medium-high speed for 2 to 3 minutes until it's light and fluffy. Slowly add the granulated sugar into the cream cheese while beating the mixture until it's well blended, scraping down the sides of the bowl as necessary. Add the marshmallow crème, mint extract and green food coloring to your liking, and continue beating until all of the ingredients are blended. Fold the prepared whipped cream and mini–chocolate chips into the filling until well combined. Pour the filling into the prepared crust. Cover and refrigerate for 2 to 4 hours until the filling firms. Once it has firmed, you can spread the chocolate pudding over the mint filling layer and return the pie to the fridge for another 2 hours to allow both layers to set together.

FOR THE TOPPING

Before serving, combine the whipping cream and powdered sugar as described above to prepare a second batch of whipped cream. Spread over the top of the pie. To garnish with chocolate shavings, run a vegetable peeler along the side of the chocolate bar to sprinkle shavings over the top of the whipped cream. Drizzle with hot fudge sauce.

easy chocolate
PUDDING PIE

When it came time to decide on a simple chocolate pudding pie, I tested several different recipes to ensure I had just the right one. The pudding needed to be just the right consistency with just the right amount of chocolate. My Easy Chocolate Pudding Pie is prepared with a classic graham cracker crust, a homemade chocolate filling and plenty of whipped cream on top. I like to garnish this pie with some simple chocolate shavings.

YIELD: 8 TO 10 SLICES

FOR THE CRUST

2 cups (180 g) graham cracker crumbs

8 tbsp (115 g) unsalted butter

FOR THE FILLING

2 large egg yolks, slightly beaten

2 tbsp (30 ml) cold water

1 tsp gelatin

2 cups (473 ml) milk

⅔ cup (128 g) granulated sugar

3 tbsp (23 g) all-purpose flour

6 oz (170 g) dark chocolate chips

FOR THE TOPPING

1 ½ cups (355 ml) heavy whipping cream

¾ cup (98 g) powdered sugar

4 oz (113 g) chocolate bar for shavings (optional)

FOR THE CRUST

Prepare a 9-inch (23-cm) springform pan by lightly greasing the edges of the pan with cooking spray, and then wiping gently with a paper towel. Before measuring, grind the graham crackers into fine crumbs using a food processor or blender. In a microwave-safe bowl, microwave the butter for 45 to 60 seconds until the butter is melted. In a separate medium-size bowl, pour the melted butter into the graham cracker crumbs and stir until there are no dry crumbs left. Pour the crumbs into your springform pan and press firmly into the bottom and up the sides to create a thick crust.

FOR THE FILLING

Measure out all of the ingredients for the filling prior to starting. Place the egg yolks in a separate bowl. In a medium-size saucepan, pour the cold water in the bottom and sprinkle the gelatin over the water and allow it to set for 2 minutes until the gelatin turns to a more solid-like consistency. Turn on the stove top to medium heat for about 30 to 60 seconds to allow the gelatin to turn back into liquid form. Once the gelatin is melted, stir in the milk and immediately add the sugar and flour, and continue to whisk aggressively to dissolve the sugar.

Once the milk mixture is warm (but not boiling), pour about ¼ cup (59 ml) of it into the bowl with the egg yolks and whisk vigorously to temper the yolks. Immediately pour the egg yolks into the saucepan and continue whisking over medium-low heat to prevent the eggs from cooking. Whisk until the pudding starts to thicken. Add the dark chocolate chips to the saucepan and whisk until they're completely melted. Remove the pan from the heat once the pudding has thickened.

(continued)

Strain the pudding through a fine sieve into the prepared pie crust. This step is optional, but it will help catch any lumps of ingredients that did not get blended. Immediately cover the top of the pudding with clear plastic wrap (directly on the surface of the pudding) and poke a few holes with a toothpick. Allow the pudding to cool on the counter for at least 1 hour before refrigerating. Refrigerate the pudding for 3 to 4 hours until the pudding has cooled and is firm.

FOR THE TOPPING

Once the pudding has completely cooled, prepare the whipped cream. Place the mixing bowl and whisk attachment in the freezer for 5 to 10 minutes to chill. Pour the heavy whipping cream into the chilled bowl and use an electric mixer to beat the heavy cream on medium-high speed until the cream gets bubbly. Slowly add the powdered sugar and continue beating on high speed until stiff peaks form. Spread the whipped cream evenly over the pie. To garnish the pie with chocolate shavings, run a vegetable peeler along the side of the chocolate bar to sprinkle shavings over the top of whipped cream.

hot mess nutella
SNICKERS PIE

My Hot Mess Nutella Snickers Pie might be the best recipe name in my whole book. The creamy Nutella filling is loaded with crushed peanuts and mini–chocolate chips. Then, it's topped with salted caramel, peanuts, whipped cream and some Snickers bar. Just like the candy bar, this pie has layers upon layers of awesomeness. I am not a regular candy eater, but when I am on the hunt for some candy, Snickers bars are at the top my list.

YIELD: 8 TO 10 SLICES

FOR THE CRUST

1 (14-oz [405-g]) package chocolate sandwich cookies (I use Oreos)

8 tbsp (115 g) unsalted butter

FOR THE FILLING

8 oz (227 g) cream cheese, softened

1 ½ cups (355 ml) heavy whipping cream

1 cup (130 g) powdered sugar

1 cup (180 g) Nutella or similar spread

½ cup (80 g) salted peanuts, chopped

½ cup (80 g) mini–chocolate chips

FOR THE TOPPING

1 cup (237 ml) heavy whipping cream

½ cup (65 g) powdered sugar

½ cup (80 g) peanuts

¼ cup (88 g) salted caramel

⅔ cup (85 g) Snickers or similar candy bar, chopped

FOR THE CRUST

Prepare a 9-inch (23-cm) springform pan by lightly greasing the edges of the pan with cooking spray, and then wiping gently with a paper towel. Grind the cookies into fine crumbs using a food processor or blender. In a microwave-safe bowl, microwave the butter for 45 to 60 seconds until the butter is melted. In a separate medium-size bowl, pour the melted butter into the cookie crumbs and stir until there are no dry crumbs left. Pour the crumbs into your springform pan and press firmly into the bottom and up the sides to create a thick crust.

FOR THE FILLING

In a large mixing bowl, beat the cream cheese at low speed for 30 seconds with the whisk attachment to eliminate any lumps. Increase the speed to medium and slowly start adding the heavy whipping cream, about ¼ cup (59 ml) at a time. The idea is to slowly add the heavy whipping cream so that the cream cheese will not be lumpy. It should resemble a liquid consistency. Once all of the heavy cream has been added, increase the speed to high until the mixture becomes bubbly. Slowly add the powdered sugar and continue beating until stiff peaks form. Turn off the mixer and spoon the Nutella into the mixing bowl. Beat the Nutella into the whipped cream slowly at first, and once it starts to mix increase the speed to medium-high and beat for 30 seconds or until stiff peaks form again. Fold the chopped peanuts and mini–chocolate chips into the batter with a spatula, and pour the filling into the prepared crust. Cover and refrigerate for 4 to 6 hours.

FOR THE TOPPING

Prepare the whipped cream by placing the mixing bowl and whisk attachment in the freezer for 5 to 10 minutes to chill. Pour the heavy whipping cream into the chilled bowl and use an electric mixer to beat the heavy cream on medium-high speed until the cream gets bubbly. Slowly add the powdered sugar and continue beating on high speed until stiff peaks form.

Remove the sides of the springform pan. Sprinkle the top of the pie with peanuts and drizzle on all but 2 tablespoons (30 ml) of the salted caramel. Pipe the whipped cream in a large circular motion, creating 10 or so peaks of whipped cream near the edge of the pie. Chop the Snickers bar into small pieces, placing a small piece on each whipped cream peak, and then pile the remaining Snickers in the middle of the pie. Drizzle with the remaining salted caramel. I suggest freezing this for 20 to 30 minutes before slicing. This will help ensure a cleaner slice. Also, I suggest using a clean, sharp knife to cut.

peanut butter
MARSHMALLOW DREAM PIE

There are a few words that come to mind when I think about this pie: light, fluffy and salty-sweet. Peanut butter is naturally salty, so to complement that, I've added some marshmallow crème and cream cheese to the filling. This is one of those pies that when you take a bite and know it's sinful, you still just can't stop. It's okay; I don't blame you. I've opted for a simple garnish of whipped cream and a sprinkle of peanuts, as the filling speaks for itself. If you love peanut butter pie, this one is for you.

YIELD: 8 TO 10 SLICES

FOR THE CRUST

1 (17-oz [470-g]) package vanilla sandwich cookies (I use Golden Oreos)

8 tbsp (115 g) unsalted butter

FOR THE FILLING

1 cup plus 2 tbsp (267 ml) heavy whipping cream, divided

½ cup (65 g) powdered sugar

4 oz (113 g) white chocolate

8 oz (227 g) cream cheese, softened

1 cup (180 g) creamy peanut butter

7 oz (198 g) marshmallow crème

FOR THE TOPPING

¾ cup (177 ml) heavy whipping cream

¼ cup (33 g) powdered sugar

2 tbsp (20 g) chopped peanuts (optional garnish)

FOR THE CRUST

Prepare a 9-inch (23-cm) springform pan by lightly greasing the edges of the pan with cooking spray, and then wiping gently with a paper towel. Grind the cookies into fine crumbs using a food processor or blender. In a microwave-safe bowl, microwave the butter for 45 to 60 seconds until the butter is melted. In a separate medium-size bowl, pour the melted butter into the cookie crumbs and stir until there are no dry crumbs left. Pour the crumbs into your springform pan and press firmly into the bottom and up the sides to create a thick crust.

FOR THE FILLING

Prepare the whipped cream first by placing a mixing bowl and whisk attachment in the freezer for 5 to 10 minutes to chill. Pour 1 cup (237 ml) heavy whipping cream into the chilled bowl and use an electric mixer to beat the heavy cream on medium-high speed until the cream gets bubbly. Slowly add the powdered sugar and continue beating on high speed until stiff peaks form. Set the whipped cream aside.

In a microwave-safe bowl, combine the white chocolate with the remaining 2 tablespoons (30 ml) heavy whipping cream and microwave in 30-second increments, stirring each time until the chocolate is melted and smooth. I suggest microwaving at 50 percent power, which helps prevent the white chocolate from seizing. Allow the chocolate to cool.

Beat the cream cheese on medium-high speed for 2 to 3 minutes until it's light and fluffy. Scrape down the sides of the bowl. Spoon the peanut butter into the cream cheese and beat on medium-high speed until it's well incorporated, scraping down the bowl as needed. Add the white chocolate and beat on medium-high speed until well mixed. Lastly, add the marshmallow crème and continue beating until all of the ingredients are blended, scraping down the sides of the bowl occasionally. Fold the prepared whipped cream into the filling until it is well combined and then pour the filling into the prepared pie crust. Cover and refrigerate for 4 hours.

FOR THE TOPPING

Combine the whipping cream and powdered sugar as described above to prepare a second batch of whipped cream. Remove the springform pan edge and use a large star tip to pipe a border on the outside edges of the cheesecake. Sprinkle the edges with chopped peanuts, if desired.

no-bake layered desserts and icebox cakes

In this chapter you'll find cookies and crackers layered with variations of pudding, whipped cream and other mousse-like creations. Once refrigerated, the cookies and crackers soften to become a cake-like texture. Layered desserts are great to serve at potlucks or other events where you need to serve a crowd. You'll find a variety of options in this chapter, from strawberries to s'mores, cookie dough to peanut butter, gingersnap and peppermint. The recipes in this chapter range from quick and simple to more difficult. There is something in here for everyone.

strawberry SHORTCAKE

I thought long and hard about how I could make the best summer-inspired no-bake dessert. Strawberry shortcake usually implies that you need to bake some sort of cake or biscuits to accompany the layers of strawberries and whipped cream. Since there is no baking allowed in my book, that wasn't going to be an option. This is where the ladyfingers come into play. Ladyfingers are the perfect substitute for a traditional shortcake because once they are soaked in orange juice, they soften just like a sponge cake. These ladyfingers are layered with a strawberry cheesecake mousse. You would never guess that adding a bit of marshmallow crème makes this filling light and fluffy.

YIELD: 9 TO 12 SLICES

FOR THE MOUSSE

¾ cups plus 2 tbsp (444 ml) heavy whipping cream, divided

1 ¼ cups (163 g) powdered sugar

12 oz (340 g) cream cheese, softened

7 oz (198 g) marshmallow crème

8 oz (226 g) fresh strawberries, divided

Zest of 1 lemon

FOR THE CRUST

1 ½ (11-oz [297-g]) packages ladyfingers

½ cup (118 ml) orange juice in bowl

FOR THE MOUSSE

Prepare the whipped cream by placing the mixing bowl and whisk attachment in the freezer for 5 to 10 minutes to chill. Pour 1 ¾ cups (414 ml) of the heavy whipping cream into the chilled bowl and use an electric mixer to beat the heavy cream on medium-high speed until the cream gets bubbly. Slowly add the powdered sugar and continue beating on high speed until stiff peaks form. Measure out ¾ cup (56 g) of whipped cream for the topping and set aside. The rest will be mixed into the mousse.

Beat the cream cheese on medium-high speed for 2 to 3 minutes until it's light and fluffy, and scrape down the sides of the bowl. Add the remaining 2 tablespoons (30 ml) of whipped cream and the marshmallow crème, and beat until well combined. In a food processor, puree 4 ounces (113 g) of strawberries and add it to the mousse. Take the remaining strawberries, chop them into small pieces and set them aside for the garnish. Mix the pureed strawberries and the zest of 1 lemon into the mousse, and beat until well combined. Lastly, fold in all but the reserved ¾ cup (56 g) of the prepared whipped topping into the mousse and mix until well combined.

FOR THE CRUST

Line the bottom of a 9-inch (23-cm) square dish that is at least 2 ½ inches (6 cm) deep with parchment paper. Dip the top of each ladyfinger into the bowl of orange juice. Line the bottom of the dish with 1 layer of dipped ladyfingers, cutting to fit if necessary. Next, evenly spread half of the mousse over the ladyfingers. Prepare the second layer of ladyfingers by again dipping the tops in the orange juice and placing them in the pan. For the last layer, spread the remaining mousse and sprinkle with the chopped strawberries. Make about 9 small whipped cream swirls on top with your reserved whipped cream and top with more strawberries, if you want. Cover and refrigerate for at least 4 hours to allow each layer to set.

apple pie LASAGNA

Since this recipe appeared on my blog it has been among my top 5 performing recipes year after year.
It starts with an easy stove top apple pie filling layered with a caramel brown sugar mousse. You may think it
sounds overly sweet, but it's balanced out with cream cheese and homemade whipped cream. This dessert is
great to prepare a day in advance, and the graham cracker softens to resemble cake.

YIELD: 12 TO 15 SLICES

FOR THE PIE FILLING

5 cups (899 g) green apples peeled and diced

2 tbsp (30 ml) fresh lemon juice

½ cup (110 g) light brown sugar

2 tbsp (16 g) all-purpose flour

1 tsp cinnamon

½ tsp apple pie spice

2 tbsp (30 ml) maple syrup

FOR THE MOUSSE FILLING

1 ¾ cups (414 ml) heavy whipping cream, divided

1 ½ cups (195 g) powdered sugar, divided

8 oz (227 g) cream cheese, softened

2 tbsp (27 g) light brown sugar

1 tsp cinnamon

½ tsp vanilla extract

2 tbsp (30 ml) caramel sauce (Hershey's or similar brand)

1 (14-oz [408-g]) box graham crackers

FOR THE TOPPING

1 ½ cups (355 ml) heavy whipping cream

¾ cup (98 g) powdered sugar

¼ cup (59 ml) caramel sauce

1 cup (170 g) toffee bits

FOR THE PIE FILLING

Place the apples into a saucepan and squeeze the fresh lemon juice over the top of the apples. Add the brown sugar, flour, cinnamon, apple pie spice and maple syrup. Stir to combine all of the ingredients. Cook the apple filling over medium-low heat, stirring occasionally for 15 to 20 minutes until the apples are softened and the filling thickens. Remove the filling from the heat and allow it to cool for 30 minutes. You can refrigerate if necessary.

FOR THE MOUSSE FILLING

Prepare the whipped cream first by placing the mixing bowl and whisk attachment in the freezer for 5 to 10 minutes to chill. Pour 1 ¼ cups (296 ml) of the heavy whipping cream into the chilled bowl and use an electric mixer to beat the heavy cream on medium-high speed until the cream gets bubbly. Slowly add ¾ cup (98 g) powdered sugar and continue beating on high speed until stiff peaks form. Set aside.

In a medium-size bowl, beat the cream cheese on medium-high speed for 2 to 3 minutes until it's light and fluffy, and scrape down the sides of the bowl. Turn off the mixer and add the remaining ¾ cup (98 g) powdered sugar, brown sugar and cinnamon. Beat at a medium speed until all of the ingredients are well combined. Add the remaining ½ cup (118 ml) of heavy whipping cream and vanilla extract. Beat on medium-high speed until the whipping cream is fully mixed into the cream cheese. Lastly, add the caramel sauce and mix it into the batter. Fold the prepared whipped cream into the cream cheese batter and divide your mousse filling into thirds.

To assemble the dessert, line a 9 × 13-inch (23 × 33-cm) pan with parchment paper. Line the bottom of the dish with 1 layer of whole graham crackers, cutting to fit as necessary. Cover the graham crackers with ⅓ of the mousse filling and spread evenly. Take half of your cooled apple pie filling and spread it over the cream cheese mousse layer, gently pressing the apple filling into the cream cheese. Add a second layer of graham crackers topped with ⅓ of the mousse and the last layer of apple pie filling. Then add a third layer of crackers and the remaining mousse. You will have 3 layers of graham crackers, 3 layers of cream cheese mousse and 2 layers of apple pie filling. The top layer will be mousse.

FOR THE TOPPING

Combine the whipping cream and powdered sugar as described above to prepare a second batch of whipped cream. Spread the whipped cream over the top layer of mousse. Drizzle caramel sauce on the whipped cream and sprinkle toffee bits on top. I prefer to add toffee bits right before serving because they will soften in the refrigerator. This lasagna needs to be refrigerated in an airtight container for at least 4 hours to allow the graham crackers to soften and the filling to set. This dessert can be prepared a day ahead of time.

birthday cake LASAGNA

My Birthday Cake Lasagna is carefully crafted for the ultimate cake batter experience. The cake batter pudding is combined with a cake batter whipped cream and cream cheese that is layered with Belgian waffle crisps. Every bite is loaded with sprinkles and cake batter filling. If you are unable to find the Belgian waffle crisps, graham crackers make a great substitute. This dessert is best when time is allowed for all of the flavors to come together; it is worth the wait!

YIELD: 12 TO 15 SLICES

FOR THE PUDDING
5 large egg yolks, slightly beaten

⅔ cup (128 g) granulated sugar

4 tbsp (31 g) vanilla cake mix

2 tbsp (19 g) cornstarch

Dash of salt

2 cups (473 ml) heavy whipping cream

½ tsp vanilla extract

FOR THE FILLING
2 cups (473 ml) heavy whipping cream

⅔ cup plus 2 tbsp (99 g) vanilla cake mix, dry

½ cup (113 g) sprinkles

8 oz (227 g) cream cheese, softened

FOR THE LAYERS
11 oz (300 g) Belgian waffle crisps

3 tbsp (43 g) sprinkles

FOR THE PUDDING
Measure out all of the ingredients for the pudding prior to starting. Place the egg yolks in a separate bowl. In a medium-size saucepan, combine sugar, vanilla cake mix, cornstarch, salt, heavy whipping cream and vanilla extract. Heat the mixture on the stove top over medium-low heat, whisking constantly to dissolve the dry ingredients in the mixture. Once the mixture is warm (but not boiling), pour about ¼ cup (59 ml) into the bowl with the egg yolks and whisk vigorously to temper the egg yolks. Immediately pour the egg yolks into the saucepan and continue whisking over medium-low heat to prevent the eggs from cooking. Whisk until the pudding starts to thicken. It will happen very quickly.

Strain the pudding through a fine sieve into a medium-size bowl. This step is optional, but it will help catch any lumps of ingredients that did not get blended. Immediately cover the top of the pudding with clear plastic wrap (directly on the surface of the pudding) and poke a few holes with a toothpick. Allow to cool on the counter for at least 1 hour before refrigerating. Refrigerate for 2 to 3 hours until the pudding has cooled and is firm.

FOR THE FILLING
Place the mixing bowl and whisk attachment in the freezer for 5 to 10 minutes to chill. Pour the heavy whipping cream into the chilled bowl and use an electric mixer to beat the heavy cream on medium-high speed until the cream gets bubbly. Slowly add the vanilla cake mix and continue beating on high speed until stiff peaks form. Next, gently fold the sprinkles into the whipped cream with a spatula. Separate out 2 cups (150 g) of the whipped cream for the filling and save the rest for the top layer of the dessert. Keep the whipped cream refrigerated while you are completing the remaining steps.

Beat the cream cheese on medium-high speed for 2 to 3 minutes until it's light and fluffy, and then scrape down the sides of the bowl. Add 1 cup (75 g) of cooled pudding into the cream cheese and beat on low speed just until combined. Lastly, add the 2 cups (150 g) of prepared whipped cream and fold it gently into the mousse using your spatula.

FOR THE LAYERS
Line the bottom of a 9-inch (23-cm) square dish at least 2 ½ inches (6 cm) tall with parchment paper. Line the bottom of the dish with 1 layer of Belgian waffle crisps, cutting if necessary. Using half of the remaining pudding, spread a thin layer of pudding over the waffle crisps. Top this layer with half of your cake batter mousse. Repeat these steps for the second layer using all of your remaining pudding and mousse. Lastly, add a third layer of waffle crisps and top with the remaining prepared whipped cream. Garnish with sprinkles. Cover and return the prepared dessert to the refrigerator for at least 3 to 4 hours to allow all of the layers to set.

cookie dough-lovers
ICEBOX CAKE

This icebox cake is a cookie dough lover's dream. Besides being stuffed with cookie dough, this dessert has layers of chocolate graham crackers and a cookie dough mousse. That's right, I said cookie dough mousse. I have been obsessed with cookie dough since I was a child and I can say, not much has changed. I should tell you though, this dessert is quite decadent, so maybe start with a smaller slice and then go back for seconds!

YIELD: 9 TO 12 SLICES

FOR THE COOKIE DOUGH

4 tbsp (57 g) unsalted butter

½ cup (96 g) granulated sugar

3 tbsp (38 g) light brown sugar

¾ cup (94 g) all-purpose flour

Dash of salt

2 tsp (10 ml) vanilla extract

1 tbsp (15 ml) milk

¼ cup (45 g) mini–chocolate chips

FOR THE MOUSSE

1 ½ cups (355 ml) heavy whipping cream

1 cup (130 g) powdered sugar

4 tbsp (31 g) all-purpose flour, divided

1 tsp vanilla extract, divided

8 oz (227 g) cream cheese, softened

¼ cup (50 g) light brown sugar

FOR THE LAYERS AND TOPPING

1 (14-oz [408-g]) box chocolate graham crackers

1 cup (237 ml) heavy whipping cream

¾ cup (98 g) powdered sugar

¼ cup (45 g) mini–chocolate chips

FOR THE COOKIE DOUGH

Start by softening the butter in the microwave for 15 seconds. In a medium-size bowl, mix the softened butter with sugar and brown sugar, and beat until it's light and fluffy. Add the flour, salt, vanilla extract and milk, and mix until the dough forms. Lastly, mix in the chocolate chips. Refrigerate the cookie dough while completing the remaining steps.

FOR THE MOUSSE

Prepare your first batch of whipped cream by chilling the mixing bowl and whisk attachment in the freezer for 5 to 10 minutes. Pour the heavy whipping cream into the chilled bowl and use an electric mixer to beat the heavy cream on medium-high speed until the cream gets bubbly. Slowly add the powdered sugar, 2 tablespoons (15 g) of flour and ½ teaspoon of vanilla extract, and continue beating on high speed until stiff peaks form. Set aside.

Beat the cream cheese on medium-high speed for 2 to 3 minutes until it's light and fluffy. Slowly add the brown sugar into the cream cheese while beating the mixture, scraping down the bowl as needed. Next, add the remaining 2 tablespoons (15 g) of flour and ½ teaspoon of vanilla extract, and beat until the filling is smooth and creamy, scraping down the sides of the bowl as needed. Fold the prepared whipped cream into this cream cheese mixture and mix until it's smooth to form your mousse.

Remove the cookie dough from the refrigerator. Roll the cookie dough into small balls, about ½ teaspoon each in size. These will be used in the layers of your icebox cake. Separate out ⅔ of your cookie dough balls.

FOR THE LAYERS AND TOPPING

To assemble the dessert, line the bottom of a 9-inch (23-cm) square dish at least 2 inches (5 cm) in height with parchment paper. Place a single layer of whole chocolate graham crackers on the bottom of the dish. Use a serrated knife to cut the graham crackers to fit if necessary. Stir ⅔ of the cookie dough balls into the mousse. Pour half of this cookie dough mousse over the graham crackers and spread evenly. Place a second layer of graham crackers and the remaining mousse, and then top with a third layer of graham crackers.

Prepare a second batch of whipped cream as described above. Spread the whipped cream over the top of the graham crackers. Sprinkle the top with the remaining ⅓ of the cookie dough balls and the mini–chocolate chips. Cover and refrigerate for at least 2 to 4 hours before serving.

S'mores LASAGNA

My S'mores Lasagna is one of the most popular recipes on my blog. Each bite is loaded with plenty of chocolate and gooey marshmallows. I love the honey flavor that the regular graham crackers add to this layered dessert, but you can certainly use all regular graham cracker or all chocolate graham crackers.

Note: I didn't want to mess too much with this recipe since it's been overwhelmingly popular, so I call for store-bought pudding and a prepared store-bought whipped topping. This helps reduce the overall preparation time because you don't have to wait for the pudding to set. I toasted the marshmallows on top with a kitchen torch but it is not a necessary step.

YIELD: 12 TO 15 SLICES

FOR THE FILLING

(3-oz [96-g]) package instant chocolate pudding

¾ cups (414 ml) milk

(8-oz [226-g]) container prepared whipped topping such as Cool Whip

oz (198 g) marshmallow crème

cup (50 g) mini-marshmallows, toasted

(14-oz [408-g]) box chocolate graham crackers

sleeve regular graham crackers

FOR THE TOPPING

cups (473 ml) heavy whipping cream

cup (130 g) powdered sugar

tbsp (14 g) cocoa powder

cups (149 g) mini-marshmallows (optional)

tbsp (30 ml) hot fudge sauce (optional)

FOR THE FILLING

Start by mixing the instant chocolate pudding with milk, and whisk until the pudding mix is dissolved. Refrigerate for about 10 minutes until firm.

In a mixing bowl, combine the whipped topping and marshmallow crème, and beat until it's smooth. Using a microwave-safe bowl, microwave the mini-marshmallows for 10 seconds, and then you have the option to use a kitchen torch with a low flame to gently toast the marshmallows. Complete the marshmallow filling by beating the melted marshmallows into the batter.

To assemble the dessert, line a 9 × 13-inch (23 × 33-cm) pan with parchment paper. Line the bottom of the dish with 1 layer of whole chocolate graham crackers, cutting to fit as necessary. Divide the marshmallow filling into thirds. Take ⅓ of the filling and spread it over the bottom layer of chocolate graham crackers. Next, spread half of the chocolate pudding on top of the marshmallow filling.

Make the next layer using regular graham crackers. Try to cover all the edges of the dish evenly. Do not break apart the larger pieces until you need to fill in the cracks. Add a second layer of marshmallow filling topped by the remaining half of the chocolate pudding. Add one last layer of chocolate graham crackers and marshmallow filling. You will have 3 layers of graham crackers, 3 layers of marshmallow filling, and 2 layers of pudding. The top layer will be marshmallow filling.

FOR THE TOPPING

Place the mixing bowl and whisk attachment in the freezer for 5 to 10 minutes to chill. Pour the heavy whipping cream into the chilled bowl and use an electric mixer to beat the heavy cream on medium-high speed until the cream gets bubbly. Slowly add the powdered sugar and cocoa powder, and continue beating on high speed until stiff peaks form. If the whipped cream is too bitter, add an additional tablespoon (8 g) of powdered sugar. Spread the whipped topping on top of the last layer of marshmallow filling.

You can top the lasagna with a layer of mini-marshmallows if you wish. You can also use a kitchen torch on low flame to gently toast the marshmallows. Do this carefully and quickly after you have placed them on top of the lasagna. I like to finish off the lasagna by drizzling hot fudge on the top layer of either the whipped topping or the toasted marshmallows, and garnishing it with leftover graham cracker crumbs. Refrigerate for 2 to 4 hours to allow each layer to set, the longer the better.

peanut butter and banana
ICEBOX CAKE

Seriously, is there any better lunch than a peanut butter and banana sandwich? When was the last time you had one of those? Not recent enough, I'll bet. This icebox cake is layers of peanut butter cookies, bananas and a peanut butter mousse. To make it even better, the cookies are dipped in milk, which helps keep them soft and cake-like. This one is for my peanut butter–loving friends. You know who you are!

YIELD: 9 SLICES

FOR THE MOUSSE

1 ¾ cups plus 2 tbsp (444 ml) heavy whipping cream, divided

2 cups (260 g) powdered sugar, divided

8 oz (227 g) cream cheese, softened

½ cup (90 g) creamy peanut butter

20 oz (567 g) peanut butter cookies (about 1 ½ packages)

½ cup (118 ml) milk in small bowl

5 medium bananas

FOR THE TOPPING

⅔ cup (158 ml) heavy whipping cream

½ cup (65 g) powdered sugar

1 tbsp (11 g) creamy peanut butter

FOR THE MOUSSE

Prepare the first batch of whipped cream by placing the mixing bowl and whisk attachment in the freezer for 5 to 10 minutes to chill. Pour 1 ¾ cups (414 ml) of heavy whipping cream into the chilled bowl and use an electric mixer to beat the heavy cream on medium-high speed until the cream gets bubbly. Slowly add 1 cup (130 g) powdered sugar and continue beating on high speed until stiff peaks form. Set aside.

Beat the cream cheese on medium-high speed for 2 to 3 minutes until it's light and fluffy, and scrape down the sides of the bowl. Add the peanut butter and remaining 2 tablespoons (30 ml) of heavy whipping cream, and continue beating until the mixture is completely smooth, scraping down the bowl occasionally. Slowly add the last cup (130 g) of powdered sugar and beat into the mixture until all of the ingredients are well combined. Fold the prepared whipped cream into the peanut butter mousse and blend with a spatula until well mixed. Divide the mousse in half.

To assemble the dessert, line the bottom of a 9-inch (23-cm) square dish at least 2 ½ inches (6 cm) tall with parchment paper. Start by dipping both sides of the peanut butter cookies into the bowl of milk. This helps soften them. Line the bottom of the dish with 1 layer of cookies, cutting to fit if necessary. Spread half of the peanut butter mousse evenly over the bottom layer of cookies. Peel and thinly slice the bananas, placing a single layer over the peanut butter mousse. Repeat the cookie layer, dipping the cookies in milk first. Then add the remaining peanut butter mousse and another layer of sliced bananas.

FOR THE TOPPING

Combine the whipping cream and powdered sugar as described above to prepare a second batch of whipped cream. Spread the whipped cream over the bananas. Lastly, microwave 1 tablespoon (11 g) of peanut butter and drizzle it over the top of the whipped cream. Cover the dessert and refrigerate for 4 to 6 hours to allow the mousse to set.

hot chocolate ICEBOX CAKE

While writing this cookbook, there were certain things I knew I wanted to include. A chocolate icebox cake was one of them. I racked my brain to find a way to make this different from a traditional chocolate icebox cake. Finally, I decided I would make a hot chocolate mousse. My hot chocolate whipped cream was the first recipe that really took off on my blog, and it was so simple! I've been making it ever since. For this recipe, I decided to add some cream cheese to create a more mousse-like texture. It is perfect for this cake because it gets firm when frozen but not quite as frozen as ice cream. If it is too cold for a frozen dessert, it can also work as a refrigerator cake!

YIELD: 8 TO 10 SLICES

FOR THE FILLING

8 oz (227 g) cream cheese, softened

¼ cup (48 g) granulated sugar

1¾ cups (414 ml) heavy whipping cream

½ cup (56 g) hot chocolate powder

FOR THE TOPPING AND LAYERS

1¼ cups (296 ml) heavy whipping cream

¾ cup (98 g) powdered sugar

1 (14-oz [408-g]) box chocolate graham crackers

½ cup (118 g) hot fudge sauce

¼ cup (113 g) sprinkles

FOR THE FILLING

Beat the cream cheese on medium-high speed for 2 to 3 minutes until it's light and fluffy, and scrape down the sides of the bowl. Add the sugar into the cream cheese while beating the mixture. Slowly pour the heavy whipping cream into the cream cheese, about ¼ cup (59 ml) at a time, and beat until the cream cheese mixture is a liquid consistency. Scrape down the bowl occasionally. Once the cream cheese is in liquid form, add the remaining heavy whipping cream and beat at a high speed until the mixture starts to thicken. Add the hot chocolate powder and beat until stiff peaks form. Set the mousse aside.

FOR THE TOPPING AND LAYERS

Place the mixing bowl and whisk attachment in the freezer for 5 to 10 minutes to chill. Pour the heavy whipping cream into the chilled bowl and use an electric mixer to beat the heavy cream on medium-high speed until the cream gets bubbly. Slowly add the powdered sugar and continue beating on high speed until stiff peaks form. Reserve 1¼ cups (94 g) of the whipped cream to pipe the edges of the cake. The rest will be spread over the top.

To assemble the dessert, line the bottom of a 9-inch (23-cm) springform pan with parchment paper, wrapping it around the removable bottom of the pan. Line the bottom of the pan with 1 layer of chocolate graham crackers, cutting to fit if necessary. If you are unable to get right to the edge, don't worry; the filling will freeze everything together. Divide the hot chocolate mousse into thirds. Spread a thin layer of mousse over the graham crackers. Repeat this step 2 more times with a layer of graham crackers and a layer of mousse to give you 3 layers of graham crackers and 3 layers of mousse. Put a final fourth layer of graham crackers on the top and cover with whipped cream. Cover and freeze for 4 hours.

Before serving, remove the edges of the springform pan. Heat the hot fudge sauce according to the instructions on the jar. Spread the hot fudge sauce over the top of the cake, pipe the border with the whipped cream you had set aside, and add the sprinkles. Return it to the freezer for 15 minutes before cutting. I suggest you cut it with a hot, serrated knife.

lemon raspberry
ICEBOX CAKE

Summertime is the perfect excuse to dig into your freezer for dessert. Homemade ice creams are great, but sometimes you want to serve a dessert with a little bit of a wow factor. This icebox cake is layers of lemon cookies, swirled lemon and raspberry mousse, and it's topped with whipped cream. You'll even find a frozen raspberry or 2 for a pop of color. The raspberry mousse is a combination of fresh raspberries, cream cheese and whipped cream. The lemon mousse is made with lemon curd, cream cheese and fresh lemon zest. I can't decide which layer I like more. Good thing I don't have to.

YIELD: 9 SLICES

FOR THE COOKIE LAYER

1 (15-oz [432-g]) package lemon sandwich cookies

8 tbsp (115 g) unsalted butter

FOR THE RASPBERRY MOUSSE LAYER

1 ½ cups (355 ml) heavy whipping cream

1 cup (130 g) powdered sugar

6 oz (170 g) raspberries, divided

4 oz (113 g) cream cheese

1 tbsp (15 ml) heavy whipping cream

FOR THE LEMON MOUSSE LAYER

8 oz (227 g) cream cheese

10 oz (284 g) lemon curd

Zest of 1 lemon

FOR THE TOPPING

1 cup (237 ml) heavy whipping cream

½ cup (65 g) powdered sugar

FOR THE COOKIE LAYER

Grind the cookies into fine crumbs using a food processor or blender. In a microwave-safe bowl, combine the cookies with butter. Microwave for 45 to 60 seconds until the butter is melted. Stir the butter into the crumbs until there are no dry crumbs left. Set the cookie mixture aside.

FOR THE RASPBERRY MOUSSE LAYER

Prepare the whipped cream by placing the mixing bowl and whisk attachment in the freezer for 5 to 10 minutes to chill. Pour the heavy whipping cream into the chilled bowl and use an electric mixer to beat the heavy cream on medium-high speed until the cream gets bubbly. Slowly add the powdered sugar and continue beating on high speed until stiff peaks form. Measure out 1 ¼ cups (94 g) of whipped cream and set aside.

Puree 2 ounces (57 g) of raspberries using a food processor or blender. Set aside. The remaining 4 ounces (113 g) of raspberries will be whole raspberries layered into the dessert. Unwrap 4 ounces (113 g) of cream cheese and soften in the microwave for 15 seconds. Beat the cream cheese on medium-high speed for 2 to 3 minutes until it's light and fluffy, and scrape down the sides of the bowl. Add the heavy whipping cream and the raspberry puree to the cream cheese. Mix on medium speed until all of the ingredients are well combined. Fold in the 1 ¼ cups (94 g) of the prepared whipped cream into the raspberry mousse until well combined. Set the mixture aside; the mousse will be divided in half to build the layers.

FOR THE LEMON MOUSSE LAYER

Unwrap 8 ounces (226 g) of cream cheese and soften in the microwave for 15 seconds. Beat the cream cheese on medium-high speed for 2 to 3 minutes until it's light and fluffy. Add the lemon curd and zest from 1 lemon into the cream cheese, and beat on medium speed until all of the ingredients are well combined, scraping the bowl as needed. Fold in the remaining prepared whipped cream until well combined. Set the mixture aside; the mousse will be divided in half to build the layers.

(continued)

lemon raspberry
ICEBOX CAKE (CONT.)

FOR THE TOPPING

Prepare a second batch of whipped cream for the topping as described on page 86.

To assemble the dessert, line the bottom of a 9-inch (23-cm) square dish at least 2 ½ inches (6 cm) tall with parchment paper. Pour half of the cookie mixture into the bottom of the pan and gently pat down. For the next layer, add half of the lemon mousse and then add half of the raspberry mousse, and use a knife to swirl the layers together. Align the remaining raspberries in rows on top of the mousse. You can either leave them whole or cut them in half. They make for a great pop of color in this dessert. If you wish, you can save a few raspberries for the final garnish.

Repeat the above steps. Add the remaining cookie mixture, and then the lemon and raspberry mousse layers swirled together with a knife. Spread the prepared whipped cream over the mousse for the top layer. Cover and freeze for 4 to 6 hours. The icebox cake will be very firm, so I suggest you remove it from the freezer at least 20 minutes before serving to soften. You can garnish with any leftover raspberries.

samoa ICEBOX CAKE

I am breaking the rules with this recipe. This is the only time I will suggest that you use your oven.
I know, I know. I just insist on having toasted coconut for my Samoa Icebox Cake. Unless of course,
you buy a package of toasted coconut. Is it required for the coconut to be toasted? Of course not,
but when I think of Samoa, I always think about toasted coconut.

Here's a few time-saving tips for this recipe. Instead of making a homemade coconut pudding, you could use
store-bought coconut pudding. Or, you can make an instant vanilla pudding, add ½ teaspoon coconut extract,
and follow the instructions on the package to finish the pudding. If you are going to make the homemade
coconut pudding (which I highly suggest you do!), just remember it needs a few hours to set,
so plan ahead or make the pudding the night before.

YIELD: 12 TO 15 SLICES

OR THE PUDDING

large egg yolks, slightly beaten

4 cup (31 g) all-purpose flour

⅔ cup (128 g) granulated sugar

2 cups (473 ml) milk

4 oz (316 g) sweetened condensed milk

tsp coconut extract

OR THE FILLING AND LAYERS

cups (151 g) coconut, divided

12 oz (340 g) cream cheese

cup (130 g) powdered sugar

½ cup (118 ml) heavy whipping cream

3 tbsp (44 ml) caramel sauce (Hershey's
or similar)

4 individual packages graham crackers
[about 1 ⅓ [14-oz (397-g)] boxes)

1 (12-oz [343-ml]) jar hot fudge sauce

OR THE TOPPING

1 ¼ cups (296 ml) heavy whipping cream

⅔ cup (87 g) powdered sugar

2 tbsp (30 ml) hot fudge sauce

2 tbsp (30 ml) caramel sauce

FOR THE PUDDING

Measure out all of the ingredients for the pudding prior to starting. Place the egg yolks
in a separate bowl. In a medium-size saucepan, add the flour and sugar, and whisk to
combine. Add the milk, sweetened condensed milk and coconut extract. Heat the mixture
on the stove top over medium-low heat. Whisk constantly to dissolve the dry ingredients.
Once the mixture is warm (but not boiling), pour about ¼ cup (59 ml) of it into the bowl
with the egg yolks and whisk vigorously to temper the egg yolks. Immediately pour the
egg yolks into the saucepan and continue whisking over medium-low heat to prevent the
eggs from cooking. Remove it from the heat as the pudding continues to thicken. It will
happen pretty quickly.

Immediately strain the pudding through a fine sieve into a medium-size bowl. This step
is optional, but it will help catch any lumps of ingredients that did not get blended.
Immediately cover the top of the pudding (directly on the pudding surface) with clear
plastic wrap, and poke a couple holes with a toothpick. Allow it to cool on the counter
for at least 1 hour before refrigerating. Refrigerate for 4 to 6 hours until the pudding has
cooled and is firm.

FOR THE FILLING AND LAYERS

Toast the coconut by preheating the oven to 400°F (200°C). Line a baking sheet with
parchment paper or a silicone mat. Spread the coconut in a single layer on the baking
sheet. Bake for 5 to 10 minutes until the coconut starts to lightly brown. Keep a close eye
on it because it can toast very quickly, depending on your oven. Remove the coconut
from the oven and allow it to cool.

(continued)

Once the pudding is firm, prepare the filling. Remove the cream cheese from the packaging and microwave for 15 seconds. Beat the softened cream cheese on medium-high speed for 2 to 3 minutes until it's light and fluffy. Slowly add the powdered sugar into the cream cheese, mixing until combined, and scrape down the sides of the bowl. Pour the heavy whipping cream slowly into the cream cheese mixture and beat until all of the ingredients are well combined. Add the caramel sauce and continue beating at medium-high speed until it's well mixed.

To assemble your icebox cake, line the bottom of a 9 × 13-inch (23 × 33-cm) dish with parchment paper. Line the bottom of the dish with 1 layer of whole graham crackers, cutting to fit if necessary. Spread half of the coconut pudding over the graham crackers. Then spread half of the caramel cream cheese filling over the pudding. Heat the hot fudge sauce in the microwave for 30 to 60 seconds, stirring occasionally. Spread 4 large spoonfuls of hot fudge sauce over the caramel cream cheese, and then sprinkle ½ cup (38 g) of toasted coconut over the hot fudge.

Build your next layer starting with graham crackers, followed by the remaining coconut pudding and caramel cream cheese filling. Then spread 4 large spoonfuls of hot fudge sauce over the last layer of filling and sprinkle ½ cup (38 g) toasted coconut over the hot fudge. Finish with a final layer of graham crackers on top.

FOR THE TOPPING

Place the mixing bowl and whisk attachment in the freezer for 5 to 10 minutes to chill. Pour the heavy whipping cream into the chilled bowl and use an electric mixer to beat the heavy cream on medium-high speed until the cream gets bubbly. Slowly add the powdered sugar and continue beating on high speed until stiff peaks form. Spread the whipped cream topping over the top layer of graham crackers. Sprinkle on all the remaining toasted coconut and drizzle with hot fudge sauce and caramel. Store covered in the refrigerator for 2 to 4 hours before serving.

tiramisu PUDDING CAKE

My Tiramisu Pudding Cake is layers of coffee liqueur and espresso-soaked ladyfingers, espresso pudding and a mascarpone mousse that will knock your socks off. You must first prepare the pudding and allow a few hours for it to set. Once it is ready, you can build this luscious dessert. If you're looking for an alcohol-free version, simply omit the coffee liqueur from the mousse and the whipped cream and replace it with coffee when you need to dip the ladyfingers.

YIELD: 9 SLICES

FOR THE PUDDING

3 large egg yolks, slightly beaten

4 tbsp (31 g) all-purpose flour

⅔ cup (128 g) granulated sugar

Dash of salt

1 cup (237 ml) milk

1 cup (237 ml) heavy whipping cream

½ cup (118 ml) strong brewed espresso

1 tsp vanilla extract

FOR THE MOUSSE AND LAYERS

8 oz (227 g) mascarpone cheese

1 cup (237 ml) heavy whipping cream

2 tbsp (30 ml) coffee liqueur such as Kahlua

½ tsp vanilla extract

1 cup (130 g) powdered sugar

¼ cup (59 ml) coffee liqueur such as Kahlua

¼ cup (59 ml) strong brewed espresso

1 ½ (11-oz [297-g]) packages ladyfingers

¼ cup (28 g) cocoa powder

FOR THE PUDDING

Measure out all of the ingredients for the pudding prior to starting. Place the egg yolks in a separate bowl. In a medium-size saucepan, add the flour, sugar and salt, and whisk to combine. Add the milk, heavy whipping cream, espresso and vanilla extract. Heat the mixture on a stove top over medium-low heat. Whisk constantly to dissolve the dry ingredients into the milk mixture. Once the mixture is warm (but not boiling), pour about ¼ cup (59 ml) of the mixture into the egg yolks and whisk vigorously to temper. Immediately pour the egg yolks into the saucepan and continue whisking over medium-low heat to prevent the eggs from cooking. Whisk until the pudding starts to thicken, and then remove it from the heat.

Strain the pudding through a fine sieve into a medium-size bowl. This step is optional, but it will help catch any lumps of ingredients that did not get properly blended. Immediately cover the top of the pudding with clear plastic wrap (directly on the surface of the pudding) and poke a few holes with a toothpick. Allow the pudding to cool on the counter for at least 1 hour before refrigerating. Refrigerate for 3 to 4 hours until the pudding has cooled and is firm. Set aside 1 cup (75 g) of the pudding to mix for the mousse.

FOR THE MOUSSE AND LAYERS

In a large mixing bowl, beat the mascarpone cheese at low speed for 30 seconds with the whisk attachment to eliminate any lumps. Increase the speed to medium and slowly start adding the heavy whipping cream, about ¼ cup (59 ml) at a time. The idea is to slowly add the whipping cream so that the mascarpone cheese will not be lumpy. It should resemble a liquid consistency. Once all of the heavy cream has been mixed in, add the coffee liqueur and vanilla extract, and increase the speed to high until the mixture becomes bubbly. Add the powdered sugar slowly and continue beating until stiff peaks form. Fold in 1 cup (75 g) of the pudding until it's well combined to form your mousse.

To assemble the dessert, line the bottom of a 9-inch (23-cm) square dish that is at least 2 ½ inches (6 cm) tall with parchment paper. Prepare a bowl combining the coffee liqueur and strong brewed espresso. Dip the top of each ladyfinger in the espresso mixture and line the bottom of the dish with 1 layer of dipped ladyfingers, cutting to fit if necessary. Next, spread half of the mousse over the ladyfingers and top with the remaining pudding, spreading evenly. Dust a thick layer of cocoa powder on top of the pudding. Prepare the next layer of ladyfingers by dipping the tops in the espresso mixture and placing them to fit in the pan as above. For the last layer, spread on the remaining mousse and sprinkle with a thick layer of cocoa powder. Cover and refrigerate for at least 2 to 4 hours to allow all of the layers to set.

black forest cheesecake
ICEBOX CAKE

There is something about combining chocolate with cherries that makes me weak at the knees. I am not the type of person to reach for a cherry-filled dessert unless it's got plenty of chocolate. The layers of this icebox cake include chocolate graham crackers and a light cherry cheesecake filling. It's topped with chocolate whipped cream, hot fudge and chocolate shavings. I like to think of this as dessert made easy because I always reach for a canned cherry pie filling. For this recipe, I've used the cherry juice in the filling as well as the whole cherries.

YIELD: 12 TO 15 SLICES

FOR THE FILLING

1¼ cups (296 ml) heavy whipping cream

¾ cup (98 g) powdered sugar

8 oz (227 g) cream cheese, softened

¼ cup (48 g) granulated sugar

5 tbsp (74 ml) cherry pie filling juice

1 cup (180 g) cherries from canned pie filling

1 (14-oz [408-g]) box chocolate graham crackers

FOR THE TOPPING

1½ cups (355 ml) heavy whipping cream

¾ cup (98 g) powdered sugar

3 tbsp (21 g) cocoa powder

4 tbsp (59 ml) hot fudge sauce

2 oz (57 g) chocolate bar for shavings

FOR THE FILLING

Prepare the whipped cream first by placing the mixing bowl and whisk attachment in the freezer for 5 to 10 minutes to chill. Pour the heavy whipping cream into the chilled bowl and use an electric mixer to beat the heavy cream on medium-high speed until the cream gets bubbly. Slowly add the powdered sugar and continue beating on high speed until stiff peaks form. Set aside.

Beat the cream cheese on medium-high speed for 2 to 3 minutes until it's light and fluffy. Add the granulated sugar, beating until well incorporated. Add the cherry pie filling juice and mix it into the cream cheese, scraping down the bowl as needed.

Next, gently fold the prepared whipped cream into the cream cheese mixture to form the cream cheese filling. Then use a slotted spoon to pull the cherries out of the juice and fold them into the filling.

To assemble your icebox cake, line the bottom of a 9 × 13-inch (23 × 33-cm) dish with parchment paper. Line the bottom of the dish with 1 layer of whole graham crackers, cutting to fit if necessary. Spread half of the cherry cream cheese filling over the graham crackers. Build your next layer starting with graham crackers, and spread the remaining filling. Top with one final layer of graham crackers.

FOR THE TOPPING

Combine the whipping cream and powdered sugar as described above to prepare a second batch of whipped cream. Add in the cocoa powder together with the powdered sugar. Spread the chocolate whipped cream over the top layer of graham crackers. Refrigerate for 4 to 6 hours to allow the graham crackers to soften and the filling to set.

Before serving, heat the hot fudge sauce in the microwave for 30 to 60 seconds until it runs off your spoon. Drizzle the hot fudge over the whipped cream. Add the chocolate shavings to the top of the cake as desired by running a vegetable peeler along the edge of the chocolate bar.

gingersnap turtle
ICEBOX CAKE

This one is for the gingerbread fans. I love the contrast between the turtle toppings and the molasses filling. Although the instructions call for this dessert to be served frozen, you can instead refrigerate it for a softer cake; however, I find that the gingersnaps get too soft and are difficult to cut through. They will stay a bit crispier if they are frozen.

For a time-saving tip, use an 8-ounce (227-g) container of store-bought whipped topping to mix into the cream cheese filling instead of making it with heavy whipping cream and powdered sugar.

YIELD: 8 TO 10 SLICES

FOR THE FILLING

8 oz (227 g) cream cheese, softened

¼ cup (48 g) granulated sugar

2 tbsp (30 ml) molasses

1 tsp cinnamon

¼ tsp cloves

1 ¾ cups (414 ml) heavy whipping cream

½ cup (65 g) powdered sugar

1 ½ (14-oz [397-g]) boxes gingersnap cookies

FOR THE TOPPING

¾ cup (177 ml) heavy whipping cream

¼ cup (33 g) powdered sugar

½ cup (50 g) pecans, crushed

3 tbsp (44 ml) hot fudge sauce

3 tbsp (44 ml) caramel sauce

Crushed gingersnaps for garnish

FOR THE FILLING

Beat the cream cheese on medium-high speed for 2 to 3 minutes until it's light and fluffy. Slowly add the sugar into the cream cheese while beating the mixture and scraping down the sides of the bowl as needed. Next, add the molasses, cinnamon and cloves, and beat until the ingredients are well mixed. Scrape down the sides of the bowl.

Next, slowly add the heavy whipping cream, about ¼ cup (59 ml) at a time until the cream cheese mixture is a liquid consistency. Then add all of the remaining heavy whipping cream and increase the speed to high. As the mixture starts to thicken, add the powdered sugar and continue beating until stiff peaks form to finish the mousse filling.

To assemble the dessert, line the bottom of a 9-inch (23-cm) springform pan with parchment paper, wrapping around the removable bottom of the pan. The pan will still close around the outside edge even if the parchment paper is hanging out. Line the bottom of the dish with 1 layer of gingersnap cookies, cutting some pieces to fit if necessary. If you are unable to get right to the edge, don't worry; the filling will freeze everything together.

Divide the mousse into fourths. Spread a thin layer of mousse over the gingersnaps. Repeat this step 3 more times with layers of gingersnaps and mousse. You should end up with 4 layers of gingersnaps and 4 layers of mousse, with a mousse layer on top. Cover the springform pan with aluminum foil and freeze for 4 hours.

FOR THE TOPPING

Place the mixing bowl and whisk attachment in the freezer for 5 to 10 minutes to chill. Pour the heavy whipping cream into the chilled bowl and use an electric mixer to beat the heavy cream on medium-high speed until the cream gets bubbly. Slowly add the powdered sugar and continue beating on high speed until stiff peaks form. Set aside.

When the cake is frozen and you are ready to serve, remove it from the freezer and remove the springform edge. You may need to run a flat-edged knife around the inside edge. Spread the crushed pecans on top of the cake. Heat the hot fudge sauce in the microwave for 30 to 60 seconds until it runs off your spoon. Drizzle the hot fudge sauce and caramel sauce over the top of the pecans. I like to use a piping bag to drizzle, but you can also use a spoon. Pipe the whipped cream around the border and sprinkle with crushed gingersnaps. Cut with a long, sharp knife to serve.

peppermint bark
ICEBOX CAKE

This is not your average peppermint ice cream dessert. It's a frozen mousse layered with chocolate graham crackers and topped with a silky whipped cream. Every bite is bursting with peppermint flavor. When frozen, the mousse remains very delicate so that you can enjoy this straight from the freezer. On top, you'll find a layer of chocolate sauce underneath the whipped cream, because you can never have enough chocolate sauce.

YIELD: 8 TO 10 SLICES

OR THE FILLING

oz (227 g) cream cheese, softened

cup (48 g) granulated sugar

¾ cups (414 ml) heavy whipping cream

tsp peppermint extract

drops red food coloring

cup (65 g) powdered sugar

cup (45 g) dark chocolate bar, chopped

(14-oz [408-g]) box chocolate graham rackers

(13-oz [245-ml]) jar hot fudge sauce

OR THE TOPPING

¼ cups (296 ml) heavy whipping cream

cup (87 g) powdered sugar

FOR THE FILLING

Beat the cream cheese on medium-high speed for 2 to 3 minutes until it's light and fluffy. Slowly add the sugar into the cream cheese while beating the mixture and scraping down the sides of the bowl as needed.

Next, slowly add the heavy whipping cream, about ¼ cup (59 ml) at a time until the cream cheese is a liquid consistency. Then add all of the remaining heavy whipping cream and increase the speed to high. As the mixture starts to thicken, add the peppermint extract, red food coloring and powdered sugar, and continue beating until stiff peaks form. Use a spatula and fold the chopped chocolate into the filling to finish your mousse.

To assemble the dessert, line the bottom of a 9-inch (23-cm) springform pan with parchment paper, wrapping around the removable bottom of the pan. The pan will still close around the outside edge even if the parchment paper is hanging out. Line the bottom of the dish with 1 layer of whole chocolate graham crackers, cutting to fit if necessary. If you are unable to get right to the edge, don't worry; the filling will freeze everything together.

Heat the hot fudge sauce according to the instructions on the jar. Save 2 tablespoons (30 ml) to drizzle on top. Divide the mousse into fourths. Spread a thin layer of mousse over the graham crackers followed by a thin layer of hot fudge sauce, about 3 tablespoons (44 ml). Repeat this step 3 more times. You should end up with 4 layers each of graham crackers, mousse and hot fudge sauce. The top layer will just be mousse.

FOR THE TOPPING

Place the mixing bowl and whisk attachment in the freezer for 5 to 10 minutes to chill. Pour the heavy whipping cream into the chilled bowl and use an electric mixer to beat the heavy cream on medium-high speed until the cream gets bubbly. Slowly add the powdered sugar and continue beating on high speed until stiff peaks form. Save 1 ½ cups (90 g) of whipped topping to pipe the edge, and spread the remaining whipped cream over top of the icebox cake.

Drizzle the remaining hot fudge sauce over the top of the whipped cream before piping the border. Cover the springform pan with aluminum foil and freeze for 4 hours. When it's frozen and you are ready to remove the springform edge, you may need to run a flat-edged knife around the inside edge of the pan. Cut with a long, sharp knife to serve.

(four)

no-bake tarts

In this chapter you'll find a mix of tarts that include pudding recipes, ganache-filled tarts and plenty of fruit-filled tarts to go around. There is chocolate, peanut butter, potato chips and even a little bit of bacon. That's right, I said it, bacon. This chapter includes single-serving desserts with a variety of mini-tart offerings. Don't stress, though. You can adapt a few of the recipes to serve a small crowd.

salty peanut butter
S'MORES TART

I've always been a sweet-and-salty girl. When it came time to make a s'mores tart, I couldn't make just any old s'mores tart. This is a salty cracker tart filled with a chocolate ganache that is loaded with peanut butter cups. It's topped with gooey melted marshmallows and drizzled with additional chocolate and peanut butter. S'mores have never looked so good.

YIELD: 8 SLICES, 9-INCH (23-CM) TART

FOR THE CRUST

¼ cups (133 g) salty cracker crumbs such as Ritz Crackers

tbsp (115 g) unsalted butter

FOR THE FILLING

0 peanut butter cups (¾ oz [21 g] each), chopped

0 oz (284 g) chocolate chips

¼ cup (177 ml) heavy whipping cream

tbsp (30 ml) corn syrup

FOR THE TOPPING

8 large marshmallows

tbsp (11 g) creamy peanut butter

oz (57 g) chocolate chips

tsp heavy whipping cream

(tip from julianne) It is best to melt the marshmallows on parchment paper or a nonstick silicon baking mat. Keep a close eye on the marshmallows, as they can puff up and melt quickly. It is best to add the melted marshmallows right before serving.

FOR THE CRUST

Before measuring, grind the crackers into fine crumbs using a food processor or blender. In a microwave-safe bowl, microwave the butter for 45 to 60 seconds until the butter is melted. In a separate medium-size bowl, pour the melted butter into the cracker crumbs and stir until there are no dry crumbs left. If you want to remove the tart from the bottom of the pan, cut a parchment circle the same size as the bottom of the pan. Pour the crumbs into a 9-inch (23-cm) tart pan and press firmly into the bottom to create a thick crust. Refrigerate the crust until the filling is ready.

FOR THE FILLING

Chop the peanut butter cups into small pieces and set aside. In a large microwave-safe bowl, combine the chocolate chips, heavy whipping cream and corn syrup. Microwave in 30-second increments until the chocolate starts to melt, stirring occasionally. Once the chocolate starts to melt, stir vigorously until the chocolate is smooth and free of lumps.

Line the bottom of the prepared crust with chopped peanut butter cups, reserving about ⅓ of the peanut butter cups for the top. Pour the filling over the chopped peanut butter cups. Sprinkle the remaining peanut butter cups over the top of the chocolate filling and gently press into the chocolate. Allow the filling to set in the refrigerator for at least 1 hour.

FOR THE TOPPING

Microwave 5 marshmallows at a time for 10 to 12 seconds each. The marshmallows will puff up slightly and start to melt on the bottom. Use 2 knives to transfer and place the marshmallows on top of the chocolate tart. Repeat these steps until the top of your tart is full of marshmallows. If you have a kitchen torch, use it to give the marshmallows a nice toasty exterior. In a microwave-safe bowl, microwave the peanut butter for 10 to 15 seconds until melted and smooth. Drizzle it over the top of the toasted marshmallows. In a microwave-safe bowl, combine the chocolate chips and the heavy whipping cream. Microwave for 20 to 30 seconds until the chocolate starts to melt, and stir until it's smooth. Drizzle the chocolate over the toasted marshmallows. Keep the tart covered and refrigerated.

raspberry margarita
CREAM TART

First of all, I love mini-desserts, and these are just the perfect single-serving size. This recipe calls for 6 mini-tart pans, but if you wish, you can use one 9-inch (23-cm) tart pan. The dessert starts off with a tequila-and-lime-infused homemade pudding, which is then mixed with whipped cream to create a soft and light mousse filling. The filling is then topped with fresh raspberries and lime zest. The contrast between the tart raspberries and the cream filling is the best part. I made these a few times during the writing of this cookbook, and each time I found it harder and harder to keep myself from sneaking bites here and there as these sat in my refrigerator. I think you will find them equally tempting!

YIELD: 6 MINI-TARTS (6 INCHES [15 CM] EACH) OR 1 LARGE TART (9 INCHES [23 CM])

FOR THE FILLING

2 large egg yolks, slightly beaten

3 tbsp (23 g) all-purpose flour

⅓ cup (63 g) granulated sugar

Dash of salt

2 ¼ cups (532 ml) heavy whipping cream, divided

Zest of 1 lime

2 tbsp (30 ml) white tequila

½ cup (65 g) powdered sugar

FOR THE CRUST

2 ½ cups (225 g) graham cracker crumbs

8 tbsp (115 g) unsalted butter

18 oz (510 g) raspberries

Zest of 1 lime

FOR THE FILLING

Measure out all of the ingredients for the filling prior to starting. Place the egg yolks in a separate bowl. In a medium-size saucepan, add the flour, granulated sugar and salt, and whisk to combine. Add 1 ¼ cups (296 ml) of heavy whipping cream and the lime zest. Heat the mixture on the stove top over medium-low heat and whisk constantly to dissolve the dry ingredients into the mixture. Once the mixture is warm (but not boiling) pour about ¼ cup (59 ml) of it into the bowl with the egg yolks and whisk vigorously to temper the egg yolks. Immediately pour the egg yolks into the saucepan and continue whisking over medium-low heat until the pudding starts to bubble and thicken. Lastly, add the tequila and vigorously whisk into the pudding; cook for an additional minute.

Pour the warm filling into a medium-size container, immediately cover the top of the pudding with clear plastic wrap (directly on the pudding surface) and poke a few holes with a toothpick. Allow the pudding to cool on the counter for at least 1 hour before refrigerating. Refrigerate for 3 to 4 hours until pudding has cooled and is firm.

Once the pudding is firm, prepare the whipped cream by placing the mixing bowl and whisk attachment in the freezer for 5 to 10 minutes to chill. Pour the remaining 1 cup (237 ml) of heavy whipping cream into the chilled bowl and use an electric mixer to beat the heavy cream on medium-high speed until the cream gets bubbly. Slowly add the powdered sugar and continue beating on high speed until stiff peaks form. Fold the whipped topping into the cooled pudding until it's smooth.

FOR THE CRUST

Before measuring, grind the graham crackers into fine crumbs using a food processor or blender. In a microwave-safe bowl, microwave the butter for 45 to 60 seconds until the butter is melted. In a separate medium-size bowl, pour the melted butter into the crumbs and stir until there are no dry crumbs left. Divide the crumbs evenly among the mini-tart pans by pouring about ½ cup (45 g) of crumbs into each 6-inch (2-cm) pan. Press firmly against the sides and bottom to form the crust.

Divide the filling among the prepared tart pans, about ½ cup (43 g) per pan. Line the raspberries on top of the filling and top with lime zest. Return the prepared tarts to the refrigerator for another 2 to 3 hours to allow the pudding to reset. Serve cold.

banana cream pie TART

There is no denying how good a slice of my Banana Cream Pie Tart is. The vanilla wafer crust is filled with vanilla pudding, sliced bananas and topped with fresh whipped cream. The homemade pudding is thicker than a traditional pudding, which complements the fresh bananas and whipped cream. This has become my go-to banana cream dessert. I prefer to add the bananas and whipped cream right before serving so they are fresh. You will need to prepare the crust and pudding in advance and allow time for the pudding to set before serving.

YIELD: 8 SLICES, 9-INCH (23-CM) TART

OR THE CRUST

¼ cups (202 g) vanilla wafer crumbs
use Nilla wafers)

tbsp (115 g) unsalted butter

OR THE PUDDING

large egg yolks, slightly beaten

tbsp (23 g) all-purpose flour

cup (64 g) granulated sugar

ash of salt

½ cups (355 ml) heavy whipping cream

tsp vanilla extract

OR THE TOPPING

large bananas, sliced

¼ cups (296 ml) heavy whipping cream

cup (98 g) powdered sugar

tbsp (30 ml) hot fudge sauce

FOR THE CRUST

Before measuring, grind the vanilla wafers into fine crumbs using a food processor or blender. In a microwave-safe bowl, microwave the butter for 45 to 60 seconds until the butter is melted. In a separate medium-size bowl, pour the melted butter into the crumbs and stir until there are no dry crumbs left. If you want to remove the tart from the bottom of the pan, cut a parchment circle the same size as the bottom of the pan. Pour the crumbs into your 9-inch (23-cm) tart pan and press firmly against the sides and bottom to form the crust.

FOR THE PUDDING

Measure out all of the ingredients for the pudding prior to starting. Place the egg yolks in a separate bowl. In a medium-size saucepan, add the flour, sugar and salt, and whisk to combine. Add the heavy whipping cream and vanilla extract. Heat the mixture on the stove top over medium-low heat and whisk constantly to dissolve the dry ingredients into the mixture. Once the mixture is warm (but not boiling), pour about ¼ cup (59 ml) of it into the bowl with the egg yolks and whisk vigorously to temper the egg yolks. Immediately pour the egg yolks into the saucepan and continue whisking over medium-low heat to prevent the eggs from cooking. Whisk until the pudding starts to thicken, and then remove it from the heat.

Immediately strain the pudding through a fine sieve into a medium-size bowl. This step is optional, but it will help catch any lumps of ingredients that did not get blended. Pour the pudding into the prepared tart crust and immediately cover the top of the pudding with clear plastic wrap (directly on the pudding surface) and poke a few holes with a toothpick. Allow the pudding to cool on the counter for at least 1 hour and then refrigerate the tart for at least 3 to 4 hours to allow the pudding to firm.

FOR THE TOPPING

Peel and thinly slice the bananas, placing them in a circular pattern over the top of the pudding starting from the outside edge and working your way into the middle. Place the mixing bowl and whisk attachment in the freezer for 5 to 10 minutes to chill. Pour the heavy whipping cream into the chilled bowl and use an electric mixer to beat the heavy cream on medium-high speed until the cream gets bubbly. Slowly add the powdered sugar and continue beating on high speed until stiff peaks form. Pipe 8 large circles of whipped cream on the outer edges of the tart or, if you wish, spread evenly over the top of the tart, covering the bananas.

Heat the hot fudge sauce in the microwave for 30 to 60 seconds until it runs off your spoon. Finish your tart by drizzling hot fudge sauce over the whipped cream. I like to use a piping bag to drizzle the hot fudge, but you can also use a spoon.

salty chocolate bacon
MINI-TARTS

These tarts were inspired by a recipe from my blog for Bacon Potato Chip Truffles. These tarts feature a salty potato chip crust filled with a chocolate ganache that includes chopped bacon bits, and it is sprinkled with sea salt. People seem to raise an eyebrow when I tell them what is in these mini-tarts, but once they take a bite, they are totally on board. And who wouldn't be, right? I prefer thick-cut maple bacon for these tarts; I just love the flavor it adds.

YIELD: 6 MINI-TARTS (4 INCHES [10 CM] EACH)

FOR THE CRUST

2 ½ cups (225 g) potato chips crumbs

3 tbsp (23 g) all-purpose flour

6 tbsp (86 g) unsalted butter

FOR THE FILLING

3 strips bacon, cooked

8 oz (227 g) dark chocolate chips

3 tbsp (44 ml) heavy whipping cream

2 tbsp (30 ml) corn syrup

1 tsp sea salt, for garnish

FOR THE CRUST

Before measuring, grind the potato chips into fine crumbs using a food processor or blender. You want to be sure there are no larger pieces because they will make the crust more difficult to hold together. Whisk the flour into the chip crumbs. In a microwave-safe bowl, microwave the butter for 45 to 60 seconds until melted. Stir the melted butter into the potato chip crumbs until there are no dry crumbs left. Gently spray the tart pans with a cooking spray. Pour the crumbs into the mini-tart pans and press firmly into the bottom and sides of the pans to create a thick crust.

Place the crusts in the freezer for 5 to 10 minutes. Remove them from the freezer and gently push the crusts from the bottom and out of the sides of tart pans. The freezing helps keep the crusts together, but if you don't loosen them from the pans, it will be more difficult to do so later on. Place the crusts back in the tart pans and prepare your filling.

FOR THE FILLING

Cook the bacon on the stove top in a large frying pan; it is better for the bacon to be crispy. Once cooked, pat them with paper towels to remove the excess grease. Chop the bacon into tiny pieces, the smaller the better. In a large microwave-safe bowl, combine the chocolate chips and the heavy whipping cream. Microwave in 30-second increments until the chocolate starts to melt. Stir the chocolate until it's completely smooth. Add the corn syrup and chopped bacon pieces and stir until well combined. Divide the filling among the prepared crusts, sprinkle the tops with sea salt and allow them to sit at room temperature for about 1 hour. Then place the mini-tarts on a sheet pan, cover with aluminum foil and refrigerate for at least 1 hour until the filling is firm. These tarts are best served at room temperature. Remove them from the refrigerator 30 minutes before serving to allow the chocolate filling to soften.

easy chocolate
MASCARPONE MOUSSE TART

This is one of those desserts that makes you lift your shoulders up, close your eyes and savor every bite. You'll never guess how easy it is to make! The filling is made with mascarpone cheese (you know, that really fancy cream cheese?), which is perfect for this mousse because it doesn't have an overbearing tangy taste like cream cheese can sometimes have. I loaded it with chocolate. It's got cocoa powder and chocolate shavings in the mousse and it's garnished with more chocolate! I am so in love with this filling that it almost didn't make it into the pan. You get my drift?

YIELD: 8 SLICES, 9-INCH (23-CM) TART

FOR THE CRUST
¼ cups (202 g) chocolate sandwich cookie crumbs (I use Oreos)
tbsp (57 g) unsalted butter

FOR THE FILLING
oz (227 g) mascarpone cheese
cups (473 ml) heavy whipping cream
cup (130 g) powdered sugar
cup (28 g) unsweetened cocoa powder
cup (50 g) chopped chocolate bar

FOR THE TOPPING
½ cups (355 ml) heavy whipping cream
cup (98 g) powdered sugar
tbsp (30 ml) hot fudge sauce for garnish
Chocolate shavings for garnish

FOR THE CRUST
Before measuring, grind the cookies into fine crumbs using a food processor or blender. In a microwave-safe bowl, microwave the butter for 45 to 60 seconds until the butter is melted. In a separate medium-size bowl, pour the melted butter into the cookie crumbs and stir until there are no dry crumbs left. If you want to remove the tart from the bottom of the pan, cut a parchment circle the same size as the bottom of the pan. Pour the crumbs into the tart pan and press firmly against the sides and bottom to form the crust.

FOR THE FILLING
In a large mixing bowl, beat the mascarpone cheese at a low speed for 30 seconds with the whisk attachment to eliminate any lumps. Increase the mixer speed to medium and slowly start adding the heavy whipping cream, about ¼ cup (59 ml) at a time. The idea is to slowly add the whipping cream so that the mascarpone cheese will not be lumpy; it should resemble a liquid consistency. Once all of the heavy cream has been added, increase the speed to high until the mixture becomes bubbly. Slowly add the powdered sugar and cocoa powder, and continue beating until stiff peaks form. Fold the chopped chocolate into your mousse filling, and then pour the mousse into the prepared crust. The mousse will tower high above your pan.

FOR THE TOPPING
Place the mixing bowl and whisk attachment in the freezer for 5 to 10 minutes to chill. Pour the heavy whipping cream into the chilled bowl and use an electric mixer to beat the heavy cream on medium-high speed until the cream gets bubbly. Slowly add the powdered sugar and continue beating on high speed until stiff peaks form. Pipe the whipped cream in a large circle motion, creating 8 or so peaks of whipped cream along the edge of the tart. Heat the hot fudge sauce in the microwave for 30 to 60 seconds, until it runs off your spoon. Drizzle the hot fudge sauce over the whipped cream. If you wish, finish your tart by sprinkling it with chocolate shavings.

cabernet spiked
CHOCOLATE TART

Nothing tops off a meal like a decadent chocolate ganache tart infused with red wine and topped with tart raspberries. Every bite of this ganache tart is meant to be savored and enjoyed slowly! The chocolate ganache is rich and creamy, so you might want to cut yourself a smaller piece. I am not much of a red wine person, unless it comes to this dessert. This is the perfect excuse to splurge a little bit.

YIELD: 10 TO 12 SLICES, 9-INCH (23-CM) TART

FOR THE CRUST

1 (14-oz [405-g]) package chocolate sandwich cookies (I use Oreos)

6 tbsp (86 g) unsalted butter

FOR THE FILLING

10 oz (284 g) dark chocolate chips

¾ cup (177 ml) heavy whipping cream

2 tbsp (30 ml) corn syrup

¼ cup (60 ml) red wine (I use a cabernet)

½ cup (75 g) raspberries

FOR THE CRUST

Grind the cookies into fine crumbs using a food processor or blender. In a microwave-safe bowl, microwave the butter for 45 to 60 seconds until the butter is melted. In a separate medium-size bowl, pour the melted butter into the cookie crumbs and stir until there are no dry crumbs left. If you want to remove the tart from the bottom of the pan, cut a parchment circle the same size as the bottom of the pan. Pour the crumbs into the tart pan and press firmly into the bottom to create a thick crust. Refrigerate the crust until the filling is ready.

FOR THE FILLING

In a large microwave-safe bowl, combine the chocolate chips, heavy whipping cream and corn syrup. Microwave in 30 second increments until the chocolate starts to melt, stirring occasionally. Once the chocolate is melted, stir vigorously until it's smooth, then add the red wine and continue mixing until well blended and the chocolate is free of lumps. Pour the filling into the prepared piecrust.

Sprinkle the raspberries over the top of the chocolate and gently press them into the chocolate. Cover the tart and refrigerate for 2 to 4 hours to allow the filling to firm.

lemon CREAM PIE TART

When it came time to decide on the flavors I wanted to include in my cookbook, lemon was a must-have item. What I love about this tart is that it is so fresh. I've incorporated lemon juice into the pudding and also added some lemon zest. I am not sure I can ever use store-bought lemon pudding again. However, store-bought pudding would be a great time-saving tip for this recipe. I've chosen to top this dessert with whipped cream. If you like meringue, it would also be wonderful with that. True lemon lovers might also enjoy this with a lemon shortbread or lemon cookie crust.

YIELD: 8 SLICES, 9-INCH (23-CM) TART

OR THE CRUST

¼ cups (202 g) shortbread cookie rumbs

tbsp (57 g) unsalted butter

OR THE PUDDING

large egg yolks, slightly beaten

tbsp (23 g) all-purpose flour

cup (64 g) granulated sugar

Dash of salt

cup (237 ml) milk

½ cup (118 ml) sweetened condensed milk

tbsp (15 ml) lemon juice

Zest of 1 large lemon

OR THE TOPPING

cup (237 ml) heavy whipping cream

½ cup (65 g) powdered sugar

2 tbsp (6 g) lemon zest

FOR THE CRUST

Before measuring, grind the cookies into fine crumbs using a food processor or blender. In a microwave-safe bowl, microwave the butter for 45 to 60 seconds until the butter is melted. In a separate medium-size bowl, pour the melted butter into the cookie crumbs and stir until there are no dry crumbs left. If you want to remove the tart from the bottom of the pan, cut a parchment circle the same size as the bottom of the pan. Pour the crumbs into the tart pan and press firmly against the sides and bottom to form the crust. Set aside.

FOR THE PUDDING

Measure out all of the ingredients for the pudding prior to starting. Egg yolks should be in a separate bowl. In a medium-size saucepan, add the flour, sugar and salt, and whisk to combine. Add the milk, sweetened condensed milk, lemon juice and lemon zest. Heat the mixture on the stove top over medium-low heat, whisking constantly to dissolve the dry ingredients into the milk mixture. Once the mixture is warm (but not boiling), pour about ¼ cup (59 ml) of it into the bowl with the egg yolks and whisk vigorously to temper the egg yolks. Immediately pour the egg yolks into the saucepan and continue whisking over medium-low heat to prevent the eggs from cooking. Whisk until the pudding starts to thicken. Once thickened, remove it from the stove top and pour the pudding into the prepared tart crust. Immediately cover the top of the pudding with clear plastic wrap (directly on the pudding surface) and poke a few holes with a toothpick. Allow the tart to cool for 30 minutes at room temperature, and then refrigerate for 3 to 4 hours until the pudding is firm.

FOR THE TOPPING

The whipped cream should be prepared right before serving for best results. Place the mixing bowl and whisk attachment in the freezer for 5 to 10 minutes to chill. Pour the heavy whipping cream into the chilled bowl and use an electric mixer to beat the heavy cream on medium-high speed until the cream gets bubbly. Slowly add the powdered sugar and continue beating on high speed until stiff peaks form. Pipe the whipped cream onto the top of the lemon tart using a large star tip and garnish with lemon zest.

german CHOCOLATE TART

There is an unexpected surprise when you bite into this German Chocolate Tart. The soft chocolate filling is a combination of German chocolate and unsweetened chocolate. German chocolate is sweeter than semi-sweet chocolate and usually contains chocolate liquor. I use the Baker's brand German chocolate, which I usually find in the baking aisle alongside the chocolate chips. This chocolate filling is spiked with bourbon and topped with pecans. The pecans have a nice buttery flavor, which complements not only the chocolate, but also the bourbon in the filling. I had the best success when I let the chocolate set at room temperature, to firm and then refrigerated it. A tart such as this is great to serve after a nice steak dinner. Just make sure you leave a little room for dessert.

YIELD: 8 SLICES, 9-INCH (23-CM) TART

FOR THE CRUST

2 ¼ cups (202 g) chocolate sandwich cookie crumbs (I use Oreos)

4 tbsp (57 g) unsalted butter

FOR THE FILLING

8 oz (227 g) German chocolate (Baker's brand or other)

2 oz (57 g) unsweetened chocolate (Baker's brand or other)

¾ cup (177 ml) heavy whipping cream

2 tbsp (30 ml) corn syrup

¼ cup (59 ml) bourbon

1 ½ cups (181 g) pecans, whole

FOR THE CRUST

Before measuring, grind the cookies into fine crumbs using a food processor or blender. In a microwave-safe bowl, microwave the butter for 45 to 60 seconds until the butter is melted. In a separate medium-size bowl, pour the melted butter into the cookie crumbs and stir until there are no dry crumbs left. If you want to remove the tart from the bottom of the pan, cut a parchment circle the same size as the bottom of the pan. Pour the crumbs into the tart pan and press firmly into the bottom to create a thick crust. Refrigerate the crust until the filling is ready.

FOR THE FILLING

In a large microwave-safe bowl, combine both the German chocolate and the unsweetened chocolate with the heavy whipping cream and corn syrup. Microwave in 30-second increments until the chocolate starts to melt, stirring occasionally. Once the chocolate is melted, stir vigorously until it's smooth. Then add the bourbon and continue mixing until well blended and the chocolate is free of lumps. Pour the filling into the prepared tart crust.

Carefully place the pecans in a circular pattern starting with the outer edge and working your way into the middle. Allow the tart to sit at room temperature for 2 to 3 hours until the filling has cooled and hardened. Refrigerating the tart can speed up the process, but the results are better when the chocolate filling is cooled to room temperature before placing it in the refrigerator.

lemon blueberry pie
MASCARPONE MINI-TART

When I think about making a pie, it's usually for a special occasion. When was the last time you made a pie just for fun? Summertime is perfect for pies, but sometimes in the summer it is too hot to turn on an oven. This is exactly the reason you need to try this recipe. It starts with a buttery shortbread crust, it is filled with a fresh blueberry pie filling, and then topped with a mascarpone whipped cream and a hint of lemon zest. The blueberry pie filling is made on the stove top and comes together rather easily. You might also consider using lemon shortbread for the crust to enhance the overall flavor of this tart. This recipe calls for 6 mini-tart pans but you can use one 9-inch (23-cm) pan instead.

YIELD: 6 MINI-TARTS (6 INCHES [15 CM]) EACH) OR 1 LARGE TART (9 INCHES [23 CM])

OR THE CRUST
½ cups (402 g) shortbread cookie umbs
tbsp (57 g) unsalted butter

OR THE FILLING
oz (510 g) fresh blueberries, rinsed
tbsp (59 ml) water
cup (96 g) granulated sugar
tbsp (11 g) all-purpose flour

OR THE TOPPING
(4-oz [113-g]) container mascarpone neese
cup (118 ml) heavy whipping cream
tbsp (24 g) powdered sugar
est of 1 lemon

FOR THE CRUST
Before measuring, grind the cookies into fine crumbs using a food processor or blender. In a microwave-safe bowl, microwave the butter for 45 to 60 seconds until the butter is melted. In a separate medium-size bowl, pour the melted butter into the cookie crumbs and stir until there are no dry crumbs left. Divide the crumbs evenly among the mini-tart pans by pouring about ½ cup (45 g) of crumbs into each pan. Press firmly against the sides and bottom to form the crust.

FOR THE FILLING
In a medium-size saucepan, combine the blueberries, water and sugar. Cook over medium-low heat, stirring occasionally. As the mixture starts to bubble, gently smash about half of the blueberries. Continue stirring while the filling is boiling for another 10 minutes. Add the flour and rapidly whisk until the flour is dissolved. Boil the filling for another few minutes until it starts to thicken. Remove it from the heat and stir occasionally. The filling will thicken as it cools. Allow it to cool at room temperature for about 30 minutes. Divide the blueberry filling among the mini-tarts, and cover each with clear plastic wrap, placing the wrap directly on the surface of the filling. Refrigerate until the filling is completely cooled.

FOR THE TOPPING
In a large mixing bowl, beat the mascarpone cheese at low speed for 30 seconds with the whisk attachment to eliminate any lumps. Increase the speed to medium and slowly start adding the heavy whipping cream, about ¼ cup (59 ml) at a time. The idea is to slowly add the whipping cream so that the mascarpone cheese will not be lumpy; it should resemble a liquid consistency. Once all of the heavy cream has been added, increase the speed to high until the mixture becomes bubbly. Slowly add the powdered sugar and continue beating until stiff peaks form. Prior to serving, divide the whipped topping among the tarts and garnish with lemon zest.

maple brown butter
APPLE MINI-TART

Apple pie is traditionally served during cookouts or after Thanksgiving dinner. I live by a few rules and one of them is that apple pie is perfect for just about any occasion. Instead of spending the time to prepare a piecrust and waiting for the pie to bake and cool, serve these quick and easy mini–apple tarts at your next get-together. My recipe uses a simple stove-top pie filling and a graham cracker crust. My favorite way to prepare apple pie is with maple syrup, lots of brown sugar and a bit of cinnamon. This recipe uses brown butter for both the crust and the apple filling. You can serve this dessert warm or cold. I love a good slice of cold apple pie myself. Make sure you get enough of the cinnamon maple whipped cream. It is the perfect way to top off this tart.

YIELD: 6 MINI-TARTS (4 INCHES [10 CM] EACH)

FOR THE CRUST

2 ½ cups (225 g) graham cracker crumbs

8 tbsp (115 g) unsalted butter

FOR THE FILLING

3 tbsp (43 g) unsalted butter

4 medium green apples

2 tsp (10 ml) lemon juice

1 tbsp (15 ml) maple syrup

2 tbsp (12 g) all-purpose flour

2 tsp (5 g) cinnamon

FOR THE TOPPING

¾ cup (177 ml) heavy whipping cream

¼ cup (33 g) powdered sugar

2 tsp (10 ml) maple syrup

1 tsp cinnamon

FOR THE CRUST

Before measuring, grind the graham crackers into fine crumbs using either a food processor or a blender. In a small saucepan, melt the butter over medium-high heat for about 2 to 3 minutes until the butter starts to turn light brown and you smell a nutty aroma. Combine the graham cracker crumbs with the browned butter, stirring the butter into the crumbs until there are no dry crumbs left.

Divide the graham cracker mixture among the 6 mini-tart pans. Each mini-tart takes just over a ½ cup (45 g). Press into the bottom and up the sides of each tart pan to form the crust. Freeze the crusts for 5 to 10 minutes while you are preparing the filling so the crusts will harden more quickly.

FOR THE FILLING

In a medium-size saucepan, melt the butter over medium-high heat for about 2 to 3 minutes until the butter starts to turn light brown and you smell a nutty aroma. Remove it from the heat and set aside. Peel and dice the apples (to about the size of a dime) into the same saucepan. Squeeze the lemon juice over the top of the apples, add the maple syrup, flour and cinnamon, and stir to combine all of the ingredients.

Cook the apple filling over medium-high heat, stirring occasionally for 12 to 15 minutes until the apples are softened and the filling thickens. Remove the filling from the heat and allow it to cool for 10 minutes. Divide the apple filling among the mini-tart pans.

FOR THE TOPPING

Place the mixing bowl and whisk attachment in the freezer for 5 to 10 minutes to chill. Pour the heavy whipping cream into the chilled bowl and use an electric mixer to beat the heavy cream on medium-high speed until the cream gets bubbly. Slowly add the powdered sugar and continue beating on high speed until soft peaks form. Lastly, add the maple syrup and cinnamon and continue beating until stiff peaks form again. Pipe the whipped cream onto the apple tarts.

(five)

ice cream and frozen treats

Ice cream isn't just a summertime treat. In this chapter you'll find enough ice cream recipes to keep you busy all year round. There is ice cream, frozen pies and cakes, ice pops and bite-size treats. Best of all, there are no special ice cream makers required. If you like boozy treats, check out the Irish Cream Frozen Mousse Cake (page 126) or the Raspberry Mojito Pops (page 134). For a new twist on a classic, take a look at the Tiramisu Ice Cream Cake (page 130) or the Oatmeal Cream Pie Ice Cream Bars (page 125). There are a total of 12 frozen desserts, one for each month. Just saying.

oatmeal cream pie
ICE CREAM BARS

There is a recipe on my blog for Oatmeal Cream Pie Ice Cream Pie, and it is pretty much dessert love at first sight. Oatmeal cream pies remind me of bagged lunches for summer camp, and I simply cannot resist them. I have adapted my ice cream pie recipe to make these homemade ice cream bars. These are much easier to make than you might think! I had the pleasure of making these with my dad when he visited us in California one summer. In exchange for the massive number of dishes he helped with during his visit, I rewarded him with a couple of these ice cream bars. He gave them 2 thumbs up. And if there's one thing about my dad, he does love his ice cream.

YIELD: 8 BARS

FOR THE ICE CREAM

½ cups plus 2 tbsp (385 ml) heavy whipping cream, divided

cup (130 g) powdered sugar

oz (227 g) cream cheese, softened

cup (101 g) light brown sugar

tsp cinnamon

tsp vanilla extract

store-bought oatmeal cream pies, chopped

FOR THE COATING

oz (340 g) dark chocolate chips

tbsp (30 ml) vegetable oil

FOR THE ICE CREAM

Prepare a batch of whipped cream first by placing your mixing bowl and whisk attachment in the freezer for 5 to 10 minutes to chill. Pour 1 ½ cups (355 ml) of heavy whipping cream into the chilled bowl and use an electric mixer to beat the heavy cream on medium-high speed until the cream gets bubbly. Slowly add the powdered sugar and continue beating on high speed until stiff peaks form. Refrigerate the whipped cream until it's ready to use.

Beat the cream cheese on medium-high speed for 2 to 3 minutes until it's light and fluffy. Slowly mix the light brown sugar and cinnamon into the cream cheese while beating, scraping down the sides of the bowl as needed. Next, add the remaining 2 tablespoons (30 ml) of heavy whipping cream and vanilla extract, and beat at a high speed for 60 seconds. Lastly, add the chopped oatmeal cream pies and beat on low speed to break up the pies, scraping down sides of the bowl as needed. Lastly, fold the chilled whipped cream into the cream cheese mixture until it's well blended to form your ice cream. Line a 9-inch (23-cm) square dish with aluminum foil, covering the bottom and the sides. Pour the ice cream mixture in the square pan, spreading it evenly, and freeze it for 2 to 3 hours until the mixture is slightly frozen but still soft enough to cut through. Remove the ice cream from the pan by lifting the edges of the aluminum foil. Peel back the edges of the aluminum foil and cut the ice cream into 8 equal bars. Place a wooden stick about ⅔ of the way into each bar and lay them flat on a sheet pan. Return the bars to the freezer for another 2 to 3 hours until they're completely firm.

FOR THE COATING

In a microwave-safe bowl, combine the chocolate chips and vegetable oil. Microwave in 30-second increments until the chocolate starts to melt, and whisk it until it's completely smooth. Pour the melted chocolate into a tall vessel that you can dip the ice cream bars into. Remove the ice cream bars one at a time from the freezer and quickly dip each bar into the chocolate and swirl it around to cover the edges. Tap off any excess chocolate. Place the coated ice cream bars in the freezer on a piece of parchment paper and allow the chocolate to freeze, then enjoy! These can be stored in the freezer for several days. You can even cut these into smaller bars to serve a crowd.

irish cream
FROZEN MOUSSE CAKE

True Irish cream fans are going to flip over this dessert. You've got to be ready for a seriously spiked piece of cake. The first layer is an Irish cream ice cream and it's topped with a chocolate mousse that is also spiked with a hint of Irish cream. It's just enough so you know it's there but not enough to overpower the chocolate flavor. I decided to garnish this cake with a simple chocolate fudge glaze since the ice cream and mousse speak for themselves. It would also be nice with a dollop of whipped cream! Grab an extra big fork and work your way through a slice.

YIELD: 1O TO 12 SLICES

FOR THE CRUST

1 (14-oz [405-g]) package chocolate sandwich cookies (I use Oreos)

8 tbsp (115 g) unsalted butter

FOR THE ICE CREAM

1 ½ cups (355 ml) heavy whipping cream

¾ cup (98 g) powdered sugar

8 oz (227 g) cream cheese, softened

½ cup (96 g) granulated sugar

⅓ cup (79 ml) Irish cream liquor such as Baileys Irish Cream

1 tsp vanilla extract

FOR THE MOUSSE

1 ½ cups (355 ml) heavy whipping cream

1 tbsp (15 ml) Irish cream liquor such as Baileys Irish Cream

½ cup (65 g) powdered sugar

2 tbsp (14 g) unsweetened cocoa powder

3 tbsp (44 ml) hot fudge sauce for garnish (optional)

FOR THE CRUST

Line the bottom of a 9-inch (23-cm) springform pan with aluminum foil, wrapping it around the removable bottom of the pan. Grind the cookies into fine crumbs using either a food processor or a blender. In a microwave-safe bowl, microwave the butter for 45 to 60 seconds until the butter is melted. In a separate medium-size bowl, pour the melted butter into the cookie crumbs and stir until there are no dry crumbs left. Pour the crumb into your springform pan and press firmly into the bottom and up the sides to create a thick crust.

FOR THE ICE CREAM

Prepare the whipped cream first by placing the mixing bowl and whisk attachment in the freezer for 5 to 10 minutes to chill. Pour the heavy whipping cream into the chilled bowl and use an electric mixer to beat the heavy cream on medium-high speed until the cream gets bubbly. Slowly add the powdered sugar and continue beating on high speed until stiff peaks form. Set aside.

Beat the cream cheese on medium-high speed for 2 to 3 minutes until it's light and fluffy. Slowly add the granulated sugar into the cream cheese while beating the mixture. Next, add the Irish cream liquor and vanilla extract. Beat until the mixture is smooth and creamy, scraping down the sides of the bowl to ensure it's well mixed. Lastly, fold the prepared whipped cream into the cream cheese until they are well combined to form your ice cream. Pour the ice cream into the prepared crust and spread it evenly.

FOR THE MOUSSE

Prepare a second batch of whipped cream in a chilled bowl as described above. Add the Irish cream liquor and beat the heavy cream until it's bubbly. Add the powdered sugar and cocoa powder and beat until stiff peaks form. Pour the mousse on top of the ice cream and spread it evenly. Cover it with parchment paper or foil and freeze for 4 to 6 hours until the ice cream is firm.

Remove it from the freezer 15 minutes before serving. When you are ready to remove the springform edge, you may need to run a flat-edged knife around the inside edge of the pan to help separate the cake. As an optional topping, heat the hot fudge according to instructions on the jar and drizzle it over the top of the cake before serving.

banana split
ICE CREAM LOAF

This dessert definitely stands out as being extra pretty to me. There are lots of flavors and textures incorporated into this ice cream loaf, just like you would see in a banana split. Everyone's favorite part about a banana split is the topping, right? This is topped with hot fudge and caramel, strawberries and cherries, and, of course, whipped cream and sprinkles. As with any banana split, garnish as you see fit.

YIELD: 6 SLICES

FOR THE ICE CREAM

cups plus 1 tbsp (370 ml) heavy
ipping cream, divided

up (130 g) powdered sugar

oz (227 g) cream cheese, softened

cup (48 g) granulated sugar

edium banana, smashed

oz (198 g) marshmallow crème

oz (85 g) dark chocolate chips

FOR THE CRUST

cups (135 g) strawberry wafer cookie
umbs

bsp (21 g) unsalted butter

FOR THE TOPPING

sp (15 ml) hot fudge sauce

bsp (15 ml) caramel sauce

edium strawberries, chopped

sp (13 g) sprinkles

araschino cherries

FOR THE ICE CREAM

To prepare the whipped cream, chill your mixing bowl and whisk attachment in the freezer for 5 to 10 minutes. Pour 1 ½ cups (355 ml) of heavy whipping cream into the chilled bowl and use an electric mixer to beat the heavy cream on medium-high speed until the cream gets bubbly. Slowly add the powdered sugar and continue beating on high speed until stiff peaks form. Save ¼ cup (19 g) of the prepared whipped cream for the topping.

Beat the cream cheese on medium-high speed for 2 to 3 minutes until the cream cheese is smooth and free of lumps. Add the granulated sugar and continue beating until it's well combined, scraping down the sides of the bowl as needed. In a small bowl, mash 1 banana into small pieces and add it to the cream cheese, beating it until it's well incorporated. Next, add the marshmallow crème and mix it on medium speed until all of the ingredients are well combined. Slowly fold the prepared whipped cream into the cream cheese mixture until it is well blended. Divide this ice cream mixture in half and place in separate bowls.

In a microwave-safe bowl, combine the chocolate chips and remaining 1 tablespoon (15 ml) of heavy whipping cream. Microwave for 30 to 60 seconds until the chocolate starts to melt, and then whisk the chocolate until it's completely smooth. Whisk the melted chocolate into ½ of the ice cream mixture to make the chocolate banana ice cream.

FOR THE CRUST

Prepare a large loaf pan by lining the sides and ends with parchment paper. Pour the vanilla-banana ice cream in the bottom of the loaf pan and then top it with the chocolate banana ice cream. This dessert will be inverted, so prepare the crust now. Before measuring, grind the strawberry wafer cookies in a food processor or blender. In a microwave-safe bowl, melt the butter for 30 to 45 seconds. Stir the butter into the wafer crumbs until there are no dry crumbs left. Pat the wafer crumbs onto the top of the chocolate banana ice cream layer. Freeze the ice cream for 4 to 6 hours.

FOR THE TOPPING

To serve, lift the ice cream out of the pan and invert it so the crust is on the bottom and peel away the parchment paper. Heat the hot fudge sauce for 30 to 60 seconds and drizzle it over the ice cream. Then drizzle with the caramel sauce and dot the top with 4 swirls of whipped cream saved from the ice cream. Garnish with cherries, diced strawberries and sprinkles or other toppings of your choice.

tiramisu ICE CREAM CAKE

I've packed all of your favorite parts of the classic tiramisu into this ice cream cake. Don't be afraid to dip your ladyfingers in the Irish cream-spiked coffee. It will soften the ladyfingers and also help keep them soft after freezing.

YIELD: 1O TO 12 SLICES

FOR THE ESPRESSO MIXTURE
1 cup (237 ml) hot water

1 tbsp (6 g) instant espresso powder

2 tbsp (30 ml) Irish cream liquor such as Baileys Irish Cream

FOR THE CHOCOLATE MOUSSE
8 oz (227 g) mascarpone cheese

1 ½ cups (355 ml) heavy whipping cream

1 tbsp (15 ml) coffee liquor (optional)

1 tsp vanilla extract

¾ cup (98 g) powdered sugar

3 tbsp (21 g) unsweetened cocoa powder

FOR THE COFFEE MOUSSE AND LAYERS
8 oz (227 g) mascarpone cheese

1 ½ cups (355 ml) heavy whipping cream

½ tsp vanilla extract

1 cup (130 g) powdered sugar

2 oz (57 g) dark chocolate bar, chopped

1 ½ (11-oz [297-g]) packages ladyfingers

¼ cup (28 g) cocoa powder

FOR THE TOPPING
¾ cup (177 ml) heavy whipping cream

¼ cup (33 g) powdered sugar

FOR THE ESPRESSO MIXTURE
In a small bowl, combine hot water and espresso powder, and whisk together until the powder is dissolved. Add the Irish cream liquor and allow the mixture to cool.

FOR THE CHOCOLATE MOUSSE
In a large mixing bowl, beat the mascarpone cheese at low speed for 30 seconds with the whisk attachment to eliminate any lumps. Increase the speed to medium and slowly start adding the heavy whipping cream about ¼ cup (59 ml) at a time. The idea is to slowly add the whipping cream so that the mascarpone cheese will not be lumpy; it should reach a liquid consistency. Once you have added all of the heavy cream, add the coffee liquor (optional) and vanilla extract, and increase the speed to high until the mixture becomes bubbly. Slowly add the powdered sugar and cocoa powder, and continue beating until stiff peaks form. Set the chocolate mousse aside.

FOR THE COFFEE MOUSSE AND LAYERS
In a large mixing bowl, beat the mascarpone cheese at low speed for 30 seconds with the whisk attachment to eliminate any lumps. Increase the speed to medium and slowly start adding the heavy whipping cream about ¼ cup (59 ml) at a time the same way as instructed above. Once you have added all of the heavy cream, add 2 tablespoons (30 ml) of the brewed espresso to the mixing bowl. Then add the vanilla extract and increase the speed to high until the mixture becomes bubbly. Slowly add the powdered sugar and continue beating until stiff peaks form. Fold the chopped chocolate bar pieces into the mousse with a spatula. Set the coffee mousse aside.

To assemble the dessert, line the bottom of a 9-inch (23-cm) springform pan with parchment paper. It's okay if it hangs over the side. Dip the top of each ladyfinger in the remaining espresso mixture and line the bottom of the dish with 1 layer of the dipped ladyfingers, cutting as necessary to fit. Next, pour the chocolate mousse over the ladyfingers, spreading it evenly. Prepare the next layer of ladyfingers by again dipping the tops in the espresso mixture and setting them atop the chocolate mousse, cutting to fit as necessary. For the last layer, spread the coffee mousse over the ladyfingers and sprinkle with a thick layer of cocoa powder. Cover and freeze for at least 2 to 4 hours to allow all of the layers to freeze.

FOR THE TOPPING
You can add the whipped topping before freezing or at the time of serving. Place the mixing bowl and whisk attachment in the freezer for 5 to 10 minutes to chill. Pour the heavy whipping cream into the chilled bowl and use an electric mixer to beat the heavy cream on medium-high speed until the cream gets bubbly. Slowly add the powdered sugar and continue beating on high speed until stiff peaks form. Use a large star tip to pipe the whipped cream along the borders of the ice cream cake.

coconut lime
ICE CREAM LOAF

This ice cream dessert combines the sweetness of coconut with some tangy lime and salty macadamia nuts. You might say it's an island-inspired dessert. I had my first key lime pie last year in Miami—yes, my first! My goal for this recipe was to incorporate all of these flavors together to create the freshest ice cream treat I could. I invite you to cut yourself a slice and relax.

YIELD: 6 TO 8 SLICES

OR THE CRUST

heaping cup (141 g) chopped macadamia
uts

cup (161 g) vanilla wafer crumbs (I use
lla wafers)

tbsp (86 g) unsalted butter

OR THE ICE CREAM

½ cups plus 2 tbsp (385 ml) heavy
hipping cream, divided

cup (130 g) powdered sugar

tsp coconut extract

oz (227 g) cream cheese, softened

cup (96 g) granulated sugar

est of 1 lime

cup (76 g) shredded sweetened coconut

FOR THE CRUST

Before measuring, use a food processor or blender to chop the macadamia nuts into small pieces. Remove the nuts from the food processor and likewise grind the vanilla wafer cookies into fine crumbs and combine them with the chopped nuts. In a microwave-safe bowl, melt the butter for 30 to 45 seconds. Stir the butter into the crust mixture until there are no dry crumbs left. Set aside 1 tablespoon (5 g) of the mixture to garnish the loaf. You will be dividing your crust into thirds to create the various layers.

FOR THE ICE CREAM

Place the mixing bowl and whisk attachment in the freezer for 5 to 10 minutes to chill. Pour 1 ½ cups (355 ml) of heavy whipping cream into the chilled bowl and use an electric mixer to beat the heavy cream on medium-high speed until the cream gets bubbly. Slowly add the powdered sugar and coconut extract, and continue beating on high until stiff peaks form. Set the whipped cream aside.

Switch to the paddle attachment on your mixer and beat the cream cheese on medium-high speed for 2 to 3 minutes until it's light and fluffy. Scrape down the sides of the bowl. Next, add the remaining 2 tablespoons (30 ml) of heavy whipping cream, the granulated sugar and the lime zest. Continue beating until all of the ingredients are well combined. Scrape down the sides and bottom of the bowl, and ensure everything is evenly mixed. Fold the prepared whipped cream into the cream cheese mixture and add the shredded coconut as you mix together the ice cream batter. Divide the ice cream into thirds.

Prepare a large loaf pan by lining the sides and ends with parchment paper. Place ⅓ of the ice cream on the bottom of the loaf pan. Next, layer on ⅓ of the crust and gently pat it into the ice cream. Add a second and a third layer of ice cream and crust, alternating the two. The top layer will be crust. Freeze the ice cream for 4 to 6 hours until it's completely firm. To serve, lift the ice cream out of pan and invert. Peel away the parchment paper and sprinkle the top with leftover coconut and macadamia nut crust that was set aside. Slice and enjoy.

raspberry MOJITO POPS

My Raspberry Mojito Pops are the perfect treat for a hot summer day. Mojitos scream summer to me. I've bottled the flavors of a traditional mojito and added raspberries to amplify the taste. As you enjoy these Popsicles, you'll have hints of lime, mint and a bit of rum, too. I made these several times until the combination was just right. The rum is subtle and not too overpowering. The raspberries offer a little bit of tartness to offset the mint flavor. It's easy to throw these pops together. The hardest part is waiting for them to freeze.

YIELD: 10 POPS

---

6 oz (170 g) raspberries

3 tbsp (85 g) granulated sugar

1 tbsp (15 ml) lime juice

6 to 8 whole small mint leaves

2 cups (473 ml) club soda

¼ cup (59 ml) white rum

10 wooden pop sticks

10 whole mint leaves (optional)

In a small food processor or blender, combine the raspberries, sugar, lime juice and mint leaves. Blend until the mixture is well combined to form a puree. In a pitcher or bowl, add the raspberry puree, club soda and white rum, and stir to combine. Pour the mixture into your ice pop molds. I recommend using a measuring cup to fill the molds to avoid spilling the liquid as you pour. Insert a wooden pop sticks and freeze for 4 hours. If you don't have the type of mold that will keep the wooden pop sticks straight, then I suggest inserting the sticks after about 1 hour of freezing. If you love mint like I do, drop a whole leaf into each pop before freezing.

candy lover's
ICE CREAM PIE

When we were growing up, we often had ice cream cakes instead of a traditional birthday cakes. They were usually alternating layers of cake and ice cream, and they were all covered with Cool Whip. These cakes were always so fun, and as I have gotten older, I have come to love experimenting with alternative birthday cakes. My Candy Lover's Ice Cream Pie is an unexpected surprise. The malted vanilla ice cream is loaded with all your favorite candies. And that's the thing—you can completely customize it with your favorite candy. I have suggested a few different candies and chocolate-coated treats, but feel free to change it up. This is the perfect excuse to get rid of that leftover Halloween candy. You might also enjoy making a chocolate version by adding 2 tablespoons (14 g) of cocoa powder to the ice cream filling.

YIELD: 8 TO 10 SLICES

FOR THE CRUST
cups (135 g) chocolate sandwich
okie crumbs (I use Oreos)

bsp (57 g) unsalted butter

FOR THE ICE CREAM
cups plus 3 tbsp (458 ml) heavy
ipping cream, divided

up (130 g) powdered sugar

oz (340 g) cream cheese, softened

cup (48 g) malt powder

sp (10 ml) vanilla extract

SUGGESTED FILLINGS
oz (57 g) Whoppers, chopped

oz (86 g) mini peanut butter cups,
opped

oz (87 g) bite-size Snickers, chopped

oz (57 g) chocolate-covered pretzels,
opped

oz (57 g) M&M's (or similar candy)

FOR THE CRUST
Line the bottom of a 9-inch (23-cm) springform pan with parchment paper, wrapping it around the removable bottom of the pan. Before measuring, grind the cookies into fine crumbs using a food processor or blender. In a microwave-safe bowl, microwave the butter for 45 to 60 seconds until the butter is melted. In a separate medium-size bowl, pour the melted butter into the cookie crumbs and stir until there are no dry crumbs left. Pour the crumbs into your springform pan and press firmly into the bottom and up the sides to create a thick crust.

FOR THE ICE CREAM
Place the mixing bowl and whisk attachment in the freezer for 5 to 10 minutes to chill. Pour 1 ¾ cups (414 ml) of heavy whipping cream into the chilled bowl and use an electric mixer to beat the heavy cream on medium-high speed until the cream gets bubbly. Slowly add the powdered sugar and continue beating on high speed until stiff peaks form. Set the whipped cream aside. Reserve 1 cup (75 g) of the prepared whipped cream to pipe a border around the pie.

Beat the cream cheese on medium-high speed for 2 to 3 minutes until it's light and fluffy. Scrape down the sides of the bowl. Add the remaining 3 tablespoons (44 ml) of heavy whipping cream, malt powder and vanilla extract. Continue beating until all of the ingredients are well combined. Lastly, fold the whipped cream into the ice cream batter until it's well mixed.

SUGGESTED FILLINGS
The candy fillings are optional and completely customizable. You can use the same flavor of candy, or you can use a variety of candies as I have done. Chop all of the candy into small pieces, about the size of your pinky finger, and fold them into your ice cream batter. Save a few pieces of each one to place on top.

Pour the filling into the prepared crust. Spread the top of the batter evenly, and then press the remaining candy pieces into the top of the ice cream. Pipe borders around the pie with whipped cream using a large piping tip. Cover and freeze the pie for 4 to 6 hours. To serve, remove the edges of the springform pan. You may need to use a flat-edged knife to help separate the springform edge from the ice cream. Cut this pie with a hot serrated knife.

no-churn snickerdoodle
COOKIE DOUGH ICE CREAM

During my first trip to Portland, Oregon, we visited a popular ice cream spot. And by visited, I mean we waited in line for 45 minutes, and then stuffed our faces with as much ice cream as we could handle. At first we thought we wouldn't be able to endure the wait, but we were so glad we did. One flavor of ice cream we ordered was cinnamon snickerdoodle ice cream. The difference between that ice cream and this one is that this recipe uses eggless cookie dough instead of baked cookies. For this recipe, I've mixed a vanilla ice cream with a cinnamon swirl and chunks of snickerdoodle cookie dough. I just can't get enough of it. Best of all, this no-churn style ice cream doesn't require any fancy ice cream makers.

YIELD: 8 SERVINGS

FOR THE COOKIE DOUGH

4 tbsp (57 g) unsalted butter

½ cup (96 g) granulated sugar

¾ cup (94 g) all-purpose flour

1 tbsp (8 g) cinnamon

2 tsp (10 ml) vanilla extract

FOR THE ICE CREAM

2 cups (473 ml) heavy whipping cream

1 cup (130 g) powdered sugar

1 tsp vanilla extract

1 (14-oz [414-ml]) can sweetened condensed milk, divided

2 tsp (5 g) cinnamon

FOR THE COOKIE DOUGH

Soften the butter in the microwave for 10 to 15 seconds. In a medium-size mixing bowl, combine the softened butter and sugar. Mix on medium speed until well combined. You may need to scrape the sides of the bowl occasionally. Once combined, add the flour, cinnamon and vanilla extract, mixing until the dough starts to thicken. Set aside.

FOR THE ICE CREAM

Prepare the whipped cream first by placing your mixing bowl and whisk attachment in the freezer for 5 to 10 minutes to chill. Pour the heavy whipping cream into the chilled bowl and use an electric mixer to beat the heavy cream on medium-high speed until the cream gets bubbly. Slowly add the powdered sugar and vanilla extract, and continue beating on high speed until stiff peaks form. Set the whipped cream aside.

Measure out and place 3 tablespoons (45 ml) of the sweetened condensed milk into a small dish and add the cinnamon. Stir until the cinnamon mixture is well combined. Set aside.

Fold the remaining sweetened condensed milk into the prepared whipped cream and use a spatula to mix it together to form your ice cream base.

Pour ⅓ of the ice cream base into a freezer-safe container. Drizzle 1 tablespoon (15 ml) of the cinnamon mixture over the ice cream and swirl it with a knife or toothpick. Break your cookie dough into small pieces and drop them into the ice cream. Don't be shy; everyone loves cookie dough. Repeat these steps 2 more times to form 3 layers of ice cream and cookie dough. You may have a little bit of leftover cookie dough. Save that for a rainy day. Just kidding! Go ahead and eat the extra; I won't tell. Cover the top with foil or parchment paper and freeze the ice cream for 4 to 6 hours until firm.

no-churn espresso bean
ICE CREAM

When I need a little pick-me-up, I like to grab a handful of chocolate-covered espresso beans. They can be quite strong if you aren't much of a coffee drinker. However, coffee lovers will adore this ice cream. The mocha ice cream is loaded with chocolate-covered espresso beans. One of my friends who tried this recipe told me the ice cream was "beautifully balanced by the bitterness of the espresso beans."

YIELD: 8 SERVINGS

oz (57 ml) hot water

sp instant espresso powder

cup (45 g) ground chocolate-covered
presso beans

cups (355 ml) heavy whipping cream

up (130 g) powdered sugar

oz (227 g) cream cheese, softened

cup (156 ml) sweetened condensed milk

In a small glass, brew the espresso by combining the hot water and espresso powder and whisk until the powder is dissolved. Set aside to allow the mixture to cool. Before measuring, grind the chocolate-covered espresso beans, in a food processor, into fine crumbs.

Place the mixing bowl and whisk attachment in the freezer for 5 to 10 minutes to chill. Pour the heavy whipping cream into the chilled bowl and use an electric mixer to beat the heavy cream on medium-high speed until the cream gets bubbly. Slowly add the powdered sugar and continue beating on high speed until stiff peaks form. Set aside.

Beat the cream cheese on medium-high speed for 2 to 3 minutes until it's light and fluffy. Scrape down the bowl and slowly add the sweetened condensed milk and brewed espresso, continuing to beat until it's well combined, scraping down the bowl as needed. Lastly, fold the whipped cream and ground espresso beans into the ice cream until it's well blended. Pour the ice cream into a freezer-safe container and freeze for 6 to 8 hours.

mocha mud pie
ICE CREAM CUPCAKES

Bass Lake near Yosemite is one of my favorite places in world. One of our must-do activities involves going to the local restaurant for its famous ice cream pie desserts. I've decided to make a mini version of their mud pie with these individual cupcakes. These ice cream cupcakes have a chocolate cookie crust with no-churn coffee ice cream and are topped with chocolate whipped cream. Make sure you grab a bite of each layer in every spoonful.

YIELD: 12 ICE CREAM CUPCAKES

FOR THE CRUST

1 ¼ cups (112 g) chocolate sandwich cookie crumbs (I use Oreos)

4 tbsp (57 g) unsalted butter

FOR THE FILLING

½ cup (118 ml) water

2 tsp (4 g) espresso powder

1 cup (237 ml) heavy whipping cream

½ cup (65 g) powdered sugar

½ cup (118 ml) sweetened condensed milk

FOR THE TOPPING

1 ¼ cups (296 ml) heavy whipping cream

½ cup (65 g) powdered sugar

2 tbsp (14 g) unsweetened cocoa powder

¼ cup (59 ml) hot fudge sauce for garnish

FOR THE CRUST

Before measuring, grind the cookies into fine crumbs using a food processor or blender. In microwave-safe bowl, microwave the butter for 45 to 60 seconds until the butter is melted. In a separate medium-size bowl, pour the melted butter into the cookie crumbs and stir until there are no dry crumbs left. Line a 12-cavity cupcake pan with cupcake liners. Spoon 1 tablespoon (5 g) of the crust into each liner and gently press down with your spoon.

FOR THE FILLING

In a microwave-safe bowl, heat the water until it boils, about 60 to 90 seconds. Add the espresso powder and mix until it's dissolved. Allow the brewed espresso to cool while you are preparing the remaining ingredients.

Prepare a batch of whipped cream by placing the mixing bowl and whisk attachment in the freezer for 5 to 10 minutes to chill. Pour the heavy whipping cream into the chilled bowl and use an electric mixer to beat the heavy cream on medium-high speed until the cream gets bubbly. Slowly add the powdered sugar and continue beating on high speed until stiff peaks form.

Pour the sweetened condensed milk into the whipped cream, turn the mixer to low speed and mix until it's combined. Measure out 4 tablespoons (59 ml) of the cooled espresso and add them to the mixture. Mix at a low speed until combined to complete your ice cream filling. Pour the filling into a large plastic bag and cut off one of the bottom corners of the bag. This basic piping bag helps add the filling to each cupcake without making a mess. Fill each cupcake liner evenly and use a knife to flatten the filling out across the top. Freeze the cupcakes for 30 to 60 minutes until they are slightly firm.

FOR THE TOPPING

Prepare a second batch of whipped cream by placing the mixing bowl and whisk attachment in the freezer for 5 to 10 minutes to chill. Pour the heavy whipping cream into the chilled bowl and use an electric mixer to beat the heavy cream on medium-high speed until the cream gets bubbly. Slowly add in the powdered sugar and cocoa powder, and continue beating on high speed until stiff peaks form. Pipe the topping onto the cupcakes Return the cupcakes to the freezer for another 3 hours until they're completely firm.

To serve, remove the wrapper. Heat the hot fudge sauce accordingly to the instructions on the jar and drizzle it over the cupcakes. They do melt very quickly, so when you take them out of the freezer, serve them right away!

hot fudge sundae CUPCAKES

These cupcakes have chocolate and vanilla together; the best of both worlds! They also have a waffle cone crust and a malted ice cream filling. For this recipe, I made 2 different varieties of the hot fudge sundae cupcake. I made a vanilla chocolate chip ice cream cupcake with chocolate whipped cream, and I also made a chocolate ice cream cupcake with vanilla whipped cream. Both the ice cream and the whipped cream are flavored with a malt powder, which adds a bit of creaminess to the ice cream.

The ingredients list and instructions below will make one full batch. If you wish to make one batch of each flavor, double the ingredients below and adjust when making either the vanilla chocolate chip ice cream cupcake or the chocolate ice cream cupcake. Feel free to garnish either of these any way you like. I drizzle on some hot fudge sauce and caramel, and add some sprinkles and a cherry on top. I like to freeze the whipped cream together with the ice cream filling, but they do melt very quickly! So when you take them out of the freezer, serve them right away.

YIELD: 1O TO 12 CUPCAKES

OR THE CRUST

up (90 g) crushed waffle cones

osp (14 g) unsalted butter

OR THE FILLING

up (237 ml) heavy whipping cream

cup (65 g) powdered sugar

cup (118 ml) sweetened condensed milk

tsp vanilla extract

bsp (14 g) malt powder

bsp (14 g) unsweetened cocoa powder

r the chocolate ice cream cupcake)

cup (90 g) mini-chocolate chips (for

th varieties)

e cups (355 ml) hot fudge sauce

OR THE TOPPING

cups (296 ml) heavy whipping cream

cup (65 g) powdered sugar

bsp (14 g) malt powder

bsp (14 g) unsweetened cocoa powder

r chocolate whipped topping)

ARNISHES (OPTIONAL)

bsp (15 ml) hot fudge sauce

bsp (15 ml) caramel sauce

bsp (15 g) sprinkles

cherries

FOR THE CRUST

Place 4 to 6 waffle cones in a large plastic bag. Use your hands to crush the cones into small pieces. In a microwave-safe bowl, combine the 1 cup (90 g) waffle crumbs with the butter. Microwave for 45 to 60 seconds until the butter is melted. Stir the butter into the crumbs. Line a cupcake pan with cupcake liners and divide the waffle crumbs evenly among them, about 1 tablespoon (5 g) per cupcake.

FOR THE FILLING

Place the mixing bowl and whisk attachment in the freezer for 5 to 10 minutes to chill. Pour the heavy whipping cream into the chilled bowl and use an electric mixer to beat the heavy cream on medium-high speed until the cream gets bubbly. Slowly add the powdered sugar and continue beating on high speed until stiff peaks form.

Pour the sweetened condensed milk, vanilla extract and malt powder into the whipped cream, turn the mixer to low speed, and mix until they're combined. If you are making the chocolate ice cream variety, add the cocoa powder at this time and mix until it's combined. Lastly, fold in the mini-chocolate chips with a spatula.

Pour the filling into a large plastic bag and cut off one of the bottom corners of the bag. The bag allows you to add the filling to each cupcake without making a mess. Fill each cupcake liner evenly. Use a knife to flatten the filling out across the top. Freeze the cupcakes for 30 to 60 minutes until they're slightly firm.

Heat the hot fudge sauce according to the instructions on the jar. Pour about 1 tablespoon (15 ml) of the hot fudge sauce over the top of the ice cream and spread it slightly. Return the cupcakes to the freezer for another 2 to 4 hours. If you want the whipped topping to be frozen, you can make it as described below and top the cupcakes after the hot fudge has been added. Otherwise, prepare it just before serving.

(continued)

hot fudge sundae
CUPCAKES (CONT.)

FOR THE TOPPING

Chill your mixing bowl and whisk attachment in the freezer for 5 to 10 minutes. Pour the whipping cream into the chilled bowl and use an electric mixer to beat on medium-high speed until the cream gets bubbly. Slowly add the powdered sugar, malt powder (and cocoa powder for the chocolate topping), and continue beating on high speed until stiff peaks form. Pipe the topping onto the cupcakes.

Prior to serving, top the ice cream cupcakes with garnishes of your choice, drizzling some hot fudge or caramel sauce, adding sprinkles and finishing them off with a cherry.

mint chocolate
ICE CREAM BITES

I love to keep my Mint Chocolate Ice Cream Bites in the freezer for times when I am craving ice cream or chocolate. There is a specialty grocery chain that makes bite-size mint chocolate ice cream sandwiches, and I love to stock up on them because I know I will be satisfied with just 1 or 2 of these. The same is true for my Mint Chocolate Ice Cream Bites. These are made in a mini-cupcake pan, which means they are the perfect size to satisfy your cravings. There are a couple of steps involved, but once you are finished, you have enough to stash away for a couple of weeks. To get the traditional green hue, just add a few drops of green food coloring to the ice cream batter.

YIELD: 24 BITES

OR THE ICE CREAM

:up (237 ml) heavy whipping cream

cup (65 g) powdered sugar

oz (113 g) cream cheese, softened

cup (118 ml) sweetened condensed milk

tsp mint extract

oz (85 g) chocolate bar, chopped

OR THE COATING

oz (326 g) chocolate chips

:o 2 tbsp (15 to 30 ml) vegetable oil

FOR THE ICE CREAM

Place the mixing bowl and whisk attachment in the freezer for 5 to 10 minutes to chill. Pour the heavy whipping cream into the chilled bowl and use an electric mixer to beat the heavy cream on medium-high speed until the cream gets bubbly. Slowly add the powdered sugar and continue beating on high speed until stiff peaks form. Set the whipped cream aside.

Beat the cream cheese on medium-high speed for 2 to 3 minutes until it's light and fluffy. Scrape down the sides of the bowl and add the sweetened condensed milk and mint extract. Beat until the mixture is well combined. Lastly, fold in the prepared whipped cream and the chocolate pieces, and mix until they're well combined to form the ice cream filling.

Line a mini-muffin pan with mini-cupcake liners. Use a spoon or small cookie scoop to fill each cup, dividing the filling evenly. You can gently tap the pan on the counter to help even out the filling inside the liners. Freeze the cupcake pan for at least 4 hours until the ice cream is firm.

Remove the pan from the freezer and quickly remove the cupcake wrappers. Place them on a half sheet pan and return them to the freezer for another 2 hours to help refreeze. The reason for this is that the no-churn ice cream melts very quickly and you want them to be completely frozen before dipping. Once these are completely frozen, prepare the dipping chocolate.

(continued)

FOR THE COATING

You will want to use a bowl narrow enough so the chocolate will be deep enough for dipping. In a microwave-safe bowl, heat the chocolate chips and 1 tablespoon (15 ml) of the vegetable oil for 60 seconds. Stir until the chocolate is completely smooth. If there are still chunks left, microwave for another 15 to 30 seconds. Test the chocolate by dipping your spoon into it. If the consistency is correct, the chocolate should easily run off the spoon. If it's still too thick, add an additional tablespoon (15 ml) of vegetable oil and whisk it into the melted chocolate.

Work in small batches, 3 to 5 pieces at a time. To dip the ice cream bites, place one on a fork and lower it into the chocolate. Use a spoon to drip the chocolate over each bite. Gently tap the fork on the side of the bowl and drag the bottom of the fork across the edge of the bowl to drip off any excess chocolate. Transfer the coated bites to a silicone mat or parchment paper to allow the chocolate to harden, and then move these pieces back to the freezer and grab a few new ones. Repeat until all the bites are covered in chocolate. Use any leftover chocolate to drizzle on the tops. Keep them frozen until they're ready to serve. These can be stored in a sealable plastic bag in your freezer.

no-bake cookies, bars and treats

This chapter has the widest variety of options for your special occasions. There is everything from quick and simple to more complex recipes. The great thing about this chapter is that not everything requires a refrigerator, so if you're prepping for a bake sale, classroom or outdoor event, you'll find this chapter helpful. These desserts also make great gifts. Some of my favorite from this chapter are the Funfetti S'more Mousse Bombs (page 153), Peanut Butter Cup Cheesecake Bars (page 164) and Espresso Bean Chocolate Truffles (page 159). Be sure to refer to my chocolate dipping tips in Chapter 8 (pages 205–215).

funfetti s'more
MOUSSE BOMBS

These bite-size treats are all about the party. These include a Birthday Cake Oreo cookie, a delicate mousse made with cream cheese and marshmallow and more Oreos. There is even a handful of sprinkles because sprinkles make everything better! To top it off, they are coated in chocolate. I love to mash-up different combinations of desserts; this one is just too much fun.

YIELD: 30 S'MORE BOMBS

R THE FILLING

up (237 ml) heavy whipping cream

cup (65 g) powdered sugar

oz (113 g) cream cheese, softened

oz (198 g) marshmallow crème

up (125 g) dry vanilla cake mix

Birthday Cake Oreo cookies (or similar okie), divided

cup (113 g) sprinkles

R THE COATING

oz (340 g) dark chocolate chips

o 2 tbsp (15 to 30 ml) vegetable oil

rinkles for garnish

FOR THE FILLING

Prepare a batch of whipped cream first by placing the mixing bowl and whisk attachment in the freezer for 5 to 10 minutes to chill. Pour the heavy whipping cream into the chilled bowl and use an electric mixer to beat the heavy cream on medium-high speed until the cream gets bubbly. Slowly add the powdered sugar and continue beating on high speed until stiff peaks form. Set the whipped cream aside.

Beat the cream cheese on medium-high speed for 2 to 3 minutes until it's light and fluffy, and scrape down the sides of the bowl as needed. Next, add the marshmallow crème and dry cake mix, and continue beating on medium speed until well combined. Crush 6 cookies in a large plastic bag such as a Ziploc bag by smashing them with a heavy kitchen tool such as a rolling pin. You will end up with a mix of fine crumbs and small pieces. Fold the crushed cookies and sprinkles into the cream cheese filling. Once mixed, fold the prepared whipped cream into the cream cheese filling.

Spread the remaining cookies on a wire rack placed over a rimmed sheet pan. Use a medium-size cookie scoop to place a spoonful of filling on top of each Oreo. Give the cookies a little tap on the counter to help the filling adhere. Place the cookies in the freezer for 30 minutes to allow the filling to become firm. After 30 minutes, prepare the chocolate coating.

FOR THE COATING

You will want to use a narrow bowl so that the chocolate is deep enough for dipping. In a microwave-safe bowl, heat the dark chocolate chips and 1 tablespoon (15 ml) of vegetable oil for 60 seconds. Stir until the chocolate is completely smooth. If there are still chunks left, microwave for another 15 to 30 seconds. Test the chocolate by dipping your spoon into it. If the consistency is correct, the chocolate should easily run off the spoon. If it's still too thick, add an additional 1 tablespoon (15 ml) of vegetable oil and whisk it into the chocolate.

(continued)

funfetti s'more
MOUSSE BOMBS (CONT.)

You have 2 options to coat the cookies in chocolate:

OPTION 1

You can dunk the cookies directly into the chocolate, tapping off any excess on the sides of the bowl and turning them upright to allow the extra chocolate to drizzle off. You will need to work quickly so the filling does not fall off.

OPTION 2

Using a spoon, drizzle the chocolate over the top of the cookies. Place the cookies on the wire rack with rimmed sheet pan beneath. With this method, there will be some run off into the pan and the cookies may not be completely coated. You may need some extra chocolate to coat them.

Garnish with sprinkles. Keep refrigerated in an airtight container until serving.

strawberry margarita
CHEESECAKE BITES

During one of my trips last summer, we stopped by a bakery that served a variety of two-bite, chocolate-covered cheesecakes. I thought I was in heaven after the first bite. I knew I needed to make some of these for my cookbook. I could not settle for just any chocolate-covered cheesecake. These cheesecake bites are loaded with fresh strawberries and lime zest. The key to making this recipe is to ensure your cheesecake is completely frozen prior to dipping them in the chocolate. After that, you can keep them in the refrigerator.

YIELD: 36 BITES

OR THE CRUST

cups (180 g) graham cracker crumbs

bsp (86 g) unsalted butter

OR THE FILLING

oz (454 g) cream cheese, softened

cup (96 g) granulated sugar

tbsp (30 ml) tequila

½ oz (92 g) strawberries, finely chopped

est of 1 lime

OR THE COATING

oz (397 g) dark chocolate chips

o 2 tbsp (15 to 30 ml) vegetable oil

FOR THE CRUST

Line the bottom of an 8-inch (20-cm) square pan with aluminum foil, wrapping it around the edges of the pan, and then line the bottom of the pan with parchment paper on top of the aluminum foil layer. Before measuring, grind the graham crackers into fine crumbs using a food processor or blender. In a microwave-safe bowl, microwave the butter for 45 to 60 seconds until the butter is melted. In a separate medium-size bowl, pour the melted butter into the graham cracker crumbs and stir until there are no dry crumbs left. Pour the crumbs into your pan and press firmly into the bottom to create a thick crust.

FOR THE FILLING

Beat the softened cream cheese on medium-high speed for 2 to 3 minutes until it's light and fluffy, scraping down the sides of the bowl as needed. Add the sugar and continue beating until it's well combined. Lastly, add the tequila, finely chopped strawberries and lime zest. Beat on a medium speed until all of the ingredients are well combined. Pour the cheesecake filling into the prepared crust and spread evenly. Freeze the cheesecake for 2 to 3 hours until firm.

Remove the cheesecake from the freezer, and use the aluminum foil to lift the cheesecake out of the pan. Slice the cheesecake into squares, 6 rows by 6 rows. Be sure the cheesecake bites are completely frozen before dipping, and remove only a few at a time to dip.

(continued)

strawberry margarita
CHEESECAKE BITES (CONT.)

FOR THE COATING

You will want to use a narrow bowl so that the chocolate is deep enough for dipping. In a microwave-safe bowl, heat the dark chocolate chips and 1 tablespoon (15 ml) of vegetable oil for 60 seconds. Stir until the chocolate is completely smooth. If there are still chunks left, microwave for another 15 to 30 seconds or until it's smooth. Test the chocolate by dipping your spoon into it. If the consistency is correct, the chocolate should easily run off the spoon. If it's still too thick, add an additional 1 tablespoon (15 ml) of vegetable oil and whisk it into the chocolate.

To dip the cheesecake bites, place one on a fork and lower it into the chocolate. Use a spoon in your other hand to drip chocolate over each square. Gently tap the fork on the sides of the bowl and drag the bottom of your fork across the edge of the bowl to drip off any excess chocolate. Transfer the dipped cheesecake to a silicone mat or parchment paper to allow the chocolate to harden. Repeat until all the pieces are covered in chocolate. Use any leftover chocolate to drizzle on top. Keep the cheesecake bites refrigerated until you are ready to serve.

espresso bean CHOCOLATE TRUFFLES

I love a good homemade food gift. Truffles are a labor of love and always seem to impress my friends. I have served these truffles on multiple occasions and they usually don't last long! I love to wrap them up in a bag or a nice tin and gift them during the holidays for someone special. The chocolate-covered espresso beans offer a burst of flavor and a little bit of crunch to the truffles. Be sure to save a couple to enjoy yourself! One of my recipe testers told me these were "so good they should be illegal."

YIELD: 36 TRUFFLES

R THE FILLING

up (237 ml) heavy whipping cream

osp (29 g) unsalted butter

oz (340 g) dark chocolate chips

cup (67 g) chocolate-covered espresso
ans

R THE COATING

oz (340 g) dark chocolate chips

to 2 tbsp (15 to 30 ml) vegetable oil

FOR THE FILLING

In a medium-size saucepan, combine the heavy whipping cream and butter. Heat on the stove top over medium heat and stir constantly until the butter is melted and the heavy cream starts to bubble (but not boil). Add the dark chocolate chips into the cream mixture and allow it to sit untouched. After 5 minutes, whisk vigorously until the chocolate is smooth. In a food processor, grind the chocolate-covered espresso beans into fine crumbs and pour into the melted chocolate, stirring until combined. Cover and refrigerate for 2 to 4 hours until the filling is firm.

Once the chocolate is firm, use a melon baller or small cookie scoop to roll the filling into balls and place on a sheet pan. Freeze for 15 to 30 minutes before dipping.

FOR THE COATING

You will want to use a narrow bowl so that the chocolate is deep enough for dipping. In a microwave-safe bowl, heat the dark chocolate chips and 1 tablespoon (15 ml) of vegetable oil for 60 seconds. Stir until the chocolate is completely smooth. If there are still chunks left, microwave for another 15 to 30 seconds. Test the chocolate by dipping your spoon into it. If the consistency is correct, the chocolate should easily run off the spoon. If it's still too thick, add an additional 1 tablespoon (15 ml) of vegetable oil and whisk it into the chocolate.

Remove the rolled truffles from the freezer in small batches to keep them from getting too soft. Stick a toothpick into the top of a truffle and swirl it in the chocolate. Tap the truffle gently on the side of the bowl to allow any excess chocolate to drip off. Place it on a piece of parchment paper and use another toothpick to help release the truffle. Repeat until all the truffles are covered. Use any excess chocolate to drizzle over the top of the truffles. Refrigerate the truffles to help the chocolate set more quickly.

monster cookie
NO-BAKE BARS

These no-bake bars are a quick snack you can throw together when the kids come home from school with their friends! Not that I have kids, but if I were a kid, I wouldn't mind these for an afterschool snack. Monster cookies are usually a combination of peanut butter, oats and M&M's. Traditionally, the cookie is flourless. However, for these bars, I chose to add some flour to the dough for stability. If you really don't want to add flour, you can substitute powdered sugar. These bars are covered with a soft chocolate ganache, so every bite is filled with chocolate and peanut butter. Is there a better combination? You can even change it up and add your own favorite candy, such as peanut butter cups. Yes! Now we're onto something.

YIELD: 9 LARGE BARS

FOR THE COOKIE DOUGH

8 tbsp (115 g) unsalted butter

½ cup (96 g) granulated sugar

¼ cup (50 g) light brown sugar

1 cup (180 g) creamy peanut butter

½ cup (62 g) all-purpose flour

1 tsp vanilla extract

2 cups (161 g) oats

¾ cup (135 g) M&M's

FOR THE TOPPING

8 oz (227 g) dark chocolate chips

3 tbsp (44 ml) heavy whipping cream

¼ cup (45 g) M&M's

FOR THE COOKIE DOUGH

Soften the butter in the microwave for 10 to 15 seconds. In a medium-size mixing bowl, combine the softened butter, granulated sugar and brown sugar. Mix at medium speed until combined. Add the peanut butter and mix together until well blended, scraping down the bowl as needed. Once combined, add the flour and vanilla extract, mixing just until the flour starts to incorporate. Slowly add the oats, 1 cup (80 g) at a time. The dough will start to thicken but continue mixing until combined. Fold the M&M's into the dough with a spatula or your hands so as not to crush the M&M's. Line a 9-inch (23-cm) square pan with parchment paper, covering the bottom and the sides. Gently push the dough into the bottom of the pan.

FOR THE TOPPING

In a medium-size microwave-safe bowl, combine the dark chocolate chips and the heavy whipping cream. Microwave in 30-second increments until the chocolate starts to melt, stirring occasionally. Once the chocolate is melted, stir vigorously until the chocolate is smooth and free of lumps. Pour the ganache over the top of the cookie dough base, spreading evenly, and sprinkle with the M&M's. Allow the ganache to set at room temperature, and then refrigerate the bars until the cookie dough and ganache harden slightly, at least 1 hour. Lift the parchment paper by the edges to remove the bars from pan before cutting.

iced animal COOKIE DOUGH BARS

Whenever I have a handful of iced animal cookies, I am immediately taken back to my childhood. These have to be the most fun cookies ever; I mean who can deny pink and white chocolate-covered cookies with sprinkles? I have made several recipes with these iced animal cookies on my blog, but this one is the easiest. Plus, you may know by this point that I love cookie dough. These cookie dough truffle bars are much easier to make than your standard truffles, and they use very similar ingredients. The cookie dough is mixed with iced animal cookies and sprinkles and topped with a layer of white chocolate and more sprinkles. If you're up for a challenge, these would make great cookie dough pops as well.

YIELD: 16 PIECES

FOR THE COOKIE DOUGH

cups (135 g) iced animal cookies, ushed

up (230 g) unsalted butter

up (192 g) granulated sugar

cup (165 g) light brown sugar

cups (281 g) all-purpose flour

tsp salt

osp (15 ml) vanilla extract

bsp (44 ml) milk

cup (57 g) sprinkles

FOR THE TRUFFLE TOPPING

oz (312 g) white chocolate chips

cup (59 ml) heavy whipping cream

osp (14 g) sprinkles

FOR THE COOKIE DOUGH

Place the iced animal cookies in a large plastic bag. Use a rolling pin to gently crush the cookies into small pieces. You want a mix of crumbs and large chunks of cookies. Soften the butter in the microwave for 10 to 15 seconds. In a medium-size mixing bowl, combine the softened butter, granulated sugar and brown sugar. Mix at medium speed until they're well combined. You may need to scrape down the bowl occasionally. Once combined, add the flour and salt, and continue mixing. The dough will be crumbly. Next, add the vanilla extract, and then mix in the milk 1 tablespoon (15 ml) at a time until the dough starts to form. Lastly, add the sprinkles and crushed animal cookies, and mix until combined to form your cookie dough.

Line a 9-inch (23-cm) square pan with parchment paper or aluminum foil and wrap it over the top edge. Empty the cookie dough into the pan and gently press the dough into the pan with your fingers.

FOR THE TRUFFLE TOPPING

In a microwave-safe bowl, combine white chocolate chips with the heavy whipping cream. Microwave at 50 percent power for 60 to 90 seconds until the chocolate starts to melt, and then whisk vigorously until the chocolate is completely smooth. Allow the chocolate to cool.

Pour the melted chocolate over the top of the cookie dough and garnish with additional sprinkles. Leave it on the counter for at least 30 minutes to allow the chocolate to cool. Then refrigerate the bars until the chocolate is cooled and firm. The chocolate will still be soft to the touch. To serve, lift the parchment paper out of the pan and cut the bars into small squares. Store in an airtight container and keep refrigerated.

peanut butter cup
CHEESECAKE BARS

One of the most popular recipes on my site is my Ultimate Reese's Peanut Butter Cup Cheesecake. It is very decadent and loaded with so much peanut butter and chocolate that I recommend only eating half a slice at a time. For this cookbook, I wanted to make a toned-down, simpler recipe that everyone can enjoy. These are still decadent and are filled with lots of peanut butter and chocolate, but they are easier to make and don't require any special equipment. These bars are perfect to take to a party. The ganache on top stays a little bit soft and it is swirled with a touch of peanut butter.

YIELD: 12 TO 15 BARS

FOR THE CRUST

1 (14-oz [405-g]) package chocolate sandwich cookies (I use Oreos)

8 tbsp (115 g) unsalted butter

FOR THE FILLING

16 oz (454 g) cream cheese, softened

2 tbsp (30 ml) heavy whipping cream

1 cup (180 g) creamy peanut butter

1 cup (130 g) powdered sugar

1 tsp vanilla extract

10 (¾ oz [21 g] each) peanut butter cups, chopped

FOR THE GANACHE

10 oz (284 g) dark chocolate chips

⅔ cup plus 1 tsp (163 ml) heavy whipping cream, divided

1 tbsp (11 g) creamy peanut butter

FOR THE CRUST

Grind the cookies into fine crumbs using a food processor or blender. In a microwave-safe bowl, microwave the butter for 45 to 60 seconds until the butter is melted. In a separate medium-size bowl, pour the melted butter into the cookie crumbs and stir until there are no dry crumbs left. Pour the crumbs into a 9 × 13-inch (23 × 33-cm) pan and press firmly into the pan to form the crust.

FOR THE FILLING

Beat the cream cheese and heavy whipping cream on medium-high speed for 2 to 3 minutes until it's light and fluffy, scraping down the bowl as needed. You want the cream cheese to appear very whipped. Next, add the peanut butter and beat on medium-high until the mixture is well combined and free of any lumps. Add the powdered sugar and vanilla extract. Slowly turn your mixture from low speed to medium high once the powdered sugar starts to incorporate. Continue beating on medium-high until all of the ingredients are well mixed. Next, fold in the chopped peanut butter cups with a spatula so the pieces don't get smashed. Pour the filling into the prepared crust and smooth out with a spatula.

FOR THE GANACHE

In a microwave-safe bowl, combine the dark chocolate chips with ⅔ cup (158 ml) of heavy whipping cream. Melt in the microwave for 30 to 60 seconds and stir the mixture until it's completely smooth. Pour your ganache over the top of the peanut butter filling and smooth out with a spatula. In a small microwave-safe bowl, combine the peanut butter with remaining 1 teaspoon heavy whipping cream. Microwave for 15 seconds and stir until it's smooth. Drizzle the peanut butter mixture over the ganache in a vertical line pattern, leaving about 1 inch (3 cm) between each line. Use a toothpick and gently drag it against the surface of the ganache in the opposite direction of the peanut butter lines. This will create a swirled pattern on top of the ganache, but be sure not to drag your toothpick too deep or you will see the toothpick lines. Refrigerate the bars for 4 hours until the filling is firm. Slice and enjoy!

salted pistachio
DARK CHOCOLATE TRUFFLES

Once I open a bag of pistachios, there is no turning back. I was surprised I had enough left to even make these truffles. When you bite into the truffles, you'll notice the texture of smooth dark chocolate contrasted with tiny pieces of pistachios. Sea salt does wonders when it's combined with chocolate, so I've sprinkled a little on top to bring out the salt in the pistachios.

YIELD: 48 TRUFFLES

FOR THE FILLING

up (237 ml) heavy whipping cream

bsp (29 g) unsalted butter

oz (340 g) dark chocolate chips

up (161 g) salted pistachios, shelled

FOR THE COATING

oz (284 g) dark chocolate chips

o 2 tbsp (15 to 30 ml) vegetable oil

sp (10 g) sea salt flakes

FOR THE FILLING

In a medium-size saucepan, add the heavy whipping cream and butter. Heat on the stove top over medium heat and stir constantly until the butter is melted and the heavy cream starts to bubble (but not boil). Add the dark chocolate chips to the cream mixture and allow it to sit untouched. After 5 minutes, whisk vigorously until the chocolate is smooth. In a food processor, grind the pistachios into fine crumbs, pour it into the melted chocolate mixture, and stir it until combined. Cover and refrigerate for 2 to 4 hours until the filling is firm.

Once the filling is firmed, use a melon baller or small cookie scoop to roll the filling into balls about 2 teaspoons (8 g) in size. Freeze for 15 to 30 minutes before dipping.

FOR THE COATING

In a microwave-safe bowl, heat the dark chocolate and 1 tablespoon (15 ml) of vegetable oil for 60 seconds. Stir it until the chocolate is completely smooth. If there are still chunks left, microwave for another 15 to 30 seconds. Test the chocolate by dipping your spoon into the chocolate. If the consistency is correct, the chocolate should easily run off the spoon. If it's still too thick, add an additional tablespoon (15 ml) of vegetable oil and whisk it into the chocolate.

Remove the rolled truffles from the freezer in small batches; it helps keep them from getting too soft. Drop 1 to 2 truffles into the chocolate and swirl them around. Use a fork to lift the truffle out of the chocolate and tap the side of the bowl to allow any excess chocolate to drip off. Place the coated truffle on a piece of parchment paper on a baking sheet and use a toothpick to release the truffle from the fork. Repeat until all of the truffles are covered with chocolate coating. Drizzle any excess chocolate over the top of the truffles and sprinkle with sea salt. Keep the truffles refrigerated.

cinnamon roll
CHEESECAKE BARS

It wasn't enough to just have a whole chapter dedicated to cheesecakes. I also needed to include some easy cheesecake bars. These classic cheesecake bars are taken up a notch with a swirled cinnamon glaze. These bars are thanks due to our obsession with snickerdoodle cookies. If I were allowed to bake for this cookbook, I would make some snickerdoodle cookies for the crust. Now we're talking. Slice up of these bars and bring them to your next potluck. You'll thank me later.

YIELD: 12 TO 15 BARS

FOR THE CRUST
2 ¼ cups (202 g) graham crackers crumbs

8 tbsp (115 g) unsalted butter

FOR THE FILLING
1 ½ cups plus 3 tbsp (399 ml) heavy whipping cream, divided

¾ cup (98 g) powdered sugar

24 oz (680 g) cream cheese, softened

⅔ cup (128 g) granulated sugar

FOR THE GLAZE
¼ cup (55 g) light brown sugar

1 tbsp (8 g) cinnamon

1 tbsp (14 g) unsalted butter

2 tsp (10 ml) heavy whipping cream

FOR THE CRUST
Before measuring, grind the graham crackers into fine crumbs using a food processor o blender. In a microwave-safe bowl, microwave the butter for 45 to 60 seconds until the butter is melted. In a separate medium-size bowl, pour the melted butter into the graha cracker crumbs and stir until there are no dry crumbs left. Pour the crumbs into a 9 × 13-inch (23 × 33-cm) pan and press firmly into the pan to form the crust.

FOR THE FILLING
Prepare the whipped cream first by placing the mixing bowl and whisk attachment in th freezer for 5 to 10 minutes to chill. Pour 1 ½ cups (355 ml) of the heavy whipping cream into the chilled bowl and use an electric mixer to beat the heavy cream on medium-high speed until the cream gets bubbly. Slowly add the powdered sugar and continue beatin on high speed until stiff peaks form. Set the whipped cream aside.

Beat the cream cheese and remaining 3 tablespoons (44 ml) of heavy whipping cream on medium-high speed for 2 to 3 minutes until it's light and fluffy, scraping down the bowl as needed. You want the cream cheese to appear very whipped. Slowly add the granulated sugar and continue beating until it's incorporated into the cream cheese mixture. Scrape th bowl and gently fold the prepared whipped cream into the cream cheese. Fold it over and over until the whipped cream is well mixed into the cheesecake filling.

FOR THE GLAZE
In a microwave-safe bowl, combine the brown sugar and cinnamon. Add the butter and microwave for 30 to 45 seconds until the butter is melted. Stir until all of the ingredients are well mixed. Add the heavy whipping cream and whisk until it's combined to form your glaze.

Divide the cheesecake filling into thirds. Spread the first third of the filling over the prepared crust. Drizzle about ⅓ of the brown sugar glaze over the cheesecake filling, an use a toothpick or knife to swirl the glaze into the cheesecake. Add a second layer of cheesecake and brown sugar glaze, again swirling it into the cheesecake. Add a third an final layer of cheesecake and glaze. Use very gentle pressure to swirl the glaze and then spread it evenly over the top with a spatula. Cover the bars and refrigerate for at least 4 hours before serving.

german chocolate
COOKIE CUPS

What's the best part about a German Chocolate Cake? It's the frosting, right? Well, these simple German Chocolate Cookie Cups eliminate the hassle of baking a cake, and allow you to jump straight to the frosting-inspired filling. Here you have mini-fillo cups, with a little bit of melted German chocolate in the bottom and a hearty scoop of coconut-pecan filling on top. These come together in about 45 minutes and can be served immediately or prepared in advance and refrigerated. They are great bite-size desserts for a cocktail party or dessert table. I use Baker's brand German chocolate, but if you cannot find that, I would suggest substituting dark chocolate.

YIELD: 30 CUPS

up plus 3 tbsp (162 ml) heavy whipping
am, divided

up (96 g) granulated sugar

osp (14 g) light brown sugar

osp (57 g) unsalted butter

osp (30 ml) corn syrup

p vanilla extract

cup (50 g) shredded sweetened
conut

cup (60 g) chopped pecans

fillo cups

z (113 g) German chocolate (Baker's
nd or similar)

In a medium-size saucepan, combine ½ cup (118 ml) of heavy whipping cream, granulated sugar, brown sugar, butter, corn syrup and vanilla extract. Cook over medium-low heat, stirring frequently until the mixture is bubbly and thickened. Remove it from the heat and stir in the coconut and pecans. Allow the mixture to sit at room temperature for 30 minutes. It will continue to thicken as it cools.

Remove the fillo cups from the packaging and place them on a plate or small sheet pan. In a microwave-safe bowl, combine the German chocolate and remaining 3 tablespoons (44 ml) of heavy whipping cream. Microwave for 30 to 60 seconds and stir until the chocolate is completely smooth. Put the chocolate in a small piping bag or plastic bag, and cut off the tip of the bag. Fill the bottom of each fillo cup with about a ½ teaspoon of chocolate. Save any remaining chocolate to drizzle on top.

Next, fill all cups with the coconut mixture. Don't be shy; there is plenty to go around. You will likely end up with some extra. I suggest you eat it with a spoon! Drizzle the remaining chocolate on the top of each cup. You can serve these right away or cover and store in the refrigerator. The chocolate will harden slightly in the refrigerator.

nutella
PEANUT BUTTER CUP DIP

Everyone needs a few go-to recipes to throw together in a bind. Whether it is a last minute company event or an upcoming party, whip up a batch of this Nutella Peanut Butter Cup Dip and serve it with a variety of cookies, crackers or pretzels. The hint of salt in the peanut butter combines so well with everyone's favorite hazelnut spread.

YIELD: ABOUT 2 CUPS (480 G)

8 oz (227 g) cream cheese, softened

⅔ cup (120 g) hazelnut spread such as Nutella

½ cup (99 g) marshmallow fluff

½ cup (65 g) powdered sugar

2 tbsp (22 g) creamy peanut butter

1 tbsp (15 ml) milk

6 peanut butter cups (¾ oz [21 g] each), chopped

Beat the cream cheese on medium-high speed for 2 to 3 minutes until it's light and fluffy, scraping down the bowl as needed. Next, add the Nutella and marshmallow fluff, and beat the mixture on medium-high speed for 2 minutes, slowly adding the powdered sugar after 1 minute. Beat until all of the ingredients are well mixed and fluffy.

In a separate microwave-safe bowl, combine the peanut butter and milk, and microwave for 20 seconds. Stir the mixture until it's smooth. Chop each peanut butter cup into 9 small pieces. To assemble the dip, make 3 layers consisting of the Nutella mixture, a handful of peanut butter cup pieces and a swirl of the peanut butter mixture. The idea is that each bite should have both Nutella and peanut butter. Serve immediately or cover and refrigerate until ready to serve. The dip will firm up in the refrigerator, so you may want to pull it out 30 minutes prior to serving to allow the dip to soften.

chocolate swirled
BUTTERFINGER DIP

I'm not saying you should take your leftover Halloween candy and use it to make this dip, but it might be a good excuse to make some candy disappear. This simple dessert dip is great with apples, or you can serve it with a variety of cookies and crackers. This is another dessert that you can whip together relatively quickly.

YIELD: ABOUT 2 CUPS (480 G)

z (227 g) cream cheese, softened

z (198 g) marshmallow fluff

up (65 g) powdered sugar

up (45 g) Butterfinger crumbs (or ilar candy), divided

ɔsp (59 ml) hot fudge sauce

Beat the cream cheese on medium-high speed for 2 to 3 minutes until it's light and fluffy, and then scrape down the sides of the bowl. Next, add the marshmallow fluff and whip on medium-high speed for 2 minutes, slowly adding the powdered sugar after 1 minute. Whip until the ingredients are well mixed and fluffy, scraping down the bowl as needed. Mix all but 1 tablespoon (11 g) of the Butterfinger crumbs into the cream cheese mixture.

Heat the hot fudge sauce according to the instructions on the jar. To assemble the dip, spoon ¼ of the cream cheese batter into the bottom of your bowl. Swirl 1 tablespoon (15 ml) of the hot fudge sauce into the cream cheese. Repeat these steps 3 more times. Sprinkle the top with the remaining Butterfinger crumbs.

Serve immediately or cover and refrigerate until ready to serve. The dip will firm up in the refrigerator, so you may want to allow it to sit at room temperature for 30 minutes prior to serving to allow the dip to soften.

cinnamon crunch BARS

My Cinnamon Crunch Bars are a great snack to prepare for a bake sale or classroom party. They come together rather quickly, and I am sure kids will love to bite into them. The base of these bars is a combination of peanut butter, powdered sugar and cinnamon cereal. It's topped with a soft chocolate ganache so every bite is a chocolate, peanut butter and cinnamon treat.

YIELD: 12 TO 15 BARS

FOR THE CRUST

3 cups (64 g) cinnamon cereal crumbs
(I like to use Cinnamon Toast Crunch)

8 tbsp (115 g) unsalted butter, melted

1 cup (180 g) creamy peanut butter

1 cup (130 g) powdered sugar

FOR THE TOPPING

8 oz (227 g) milk chocolate chips

½ cup plus 1 tbsp (133 ml) heavy whipping cream, divided

2 oz (57 g) white chocolate

½ cup (11 g) cinnamon cereal (I like to use Cinnamon Toast Crunch) for garnish

FOR THE CRUST

Before measuring, grind the cinnamon cereal into fine crumbs using a food processor or blender. In a large mixing bowl, combine the crumbs with melted butter and peanut butter, and beat together until the ingredients are well combined. Reduce the mixing speed and slowly add the powdered sugar, beating until all of the ingredients are well mixed. Pour the mixture into a 9-inch (23-cm) square pan and press firmly into the pan to form the crust. Refrigerate for 30 minutes to allow the crust to firm.

FOR THE TOPPING

In a microwave-safe bowl, combine the milk chocolate chips with ½ cup (118 ml) of heavy whipping cream. Microwave for 30 to 60 seconds until the chocolate starts to melt, and then whisk thoroughly until the milk chocolate is smooth.

In a separate microwave-safe bowl, combine the white chocolate with remaining 1 tablespoon (15 ml) heavy whipping cream. Microwave for 30 to 60 seconds until the chocolate starts to melt. I suggest microwaving at 50 percent power, which helps prevent the white chocolate from seizing. Whisk thoroughly until the white chocolate mixture is smooth. Allow the white chocolate to cool.

Pour ¾ of the melted milk chocolate over the prepared crust and spread evenly with a spatula. Next, swirl in the white chocolate by drizzling half of it over the milk chocolate and swirling with a knife. Repeat these steps with all of the remaining melted chocolate, swirling together on top with a knife. Sprinkle the cinnamon cereal over the top and gently press into the chocolate. Allow the chocolate to cool to room temperature (for about 30 minutes), and then refrigerate it for an hour. Keep it covered and refrigerated until ready to serve. Slice before serving.

coconut lime
COOKIE TRUFFLES

My Coconut Lime Cookie Truffles are a refreshing treat to pop in your mouth on those hot summer days! Truffles and I are what I like to call frenemies. I won't sit here and tell you how easy it is to make truffles, because I am never quite happy with how the truffles look. I am always looking at truffle recipes from my friends with such envy! This is why I also like to cover my truffles with a drizzle of chocolate or in this case a sprinkle of graham crackers. It helps to cover up any unwanted spots! It also helps to freeze your truffles before dipping, and then you can give them a quick roll between your palms to give them a smoother shape. Even though we're not always friends at the start, I forget about all of the work I put into making the truffles once I am shoving them in my mouth left and right!

YIELD: 45 TO 50 TRUFFLES

FOR THE FILLING

(15-oz [432-g]) package vanilla sandwich
cookies (I use Golden Oreos)

½ cups (135 g) graham cracker crumbs

oz (227 g) cream cheese, softened

est of 2 limes

cups (151 g) shredded sweetened
coconut

FOR THE COATING

oz (454 g) white chocolate chips

tbsp (55 g) vegetable shortening

est of 1 lime

cup (48 g) graham cracker crumbs

FOR THE FILLING

Grind the vanilla cookies into fine crumbs using a food processor or blender. Repeat the same step for the graham crackers as needed. Mix together in a medium-size bowl and set aside.

In a large bowl, beat the cream cheese on medium-high speed for 2 to 3 minutes until it's light and fluffy. Zest 2 limes into the cream cheese and continue beating until it's well mixed. Scrape down the sides of the bowl and add the shredded coconut and cookie crumb mixture. Beat on medium speed until all of the ingredients are well combined.

Using a small cookie scoop (about the size of 1 tablespoon [15 g]), scoop the filling onto a pan lined with parchment paper. Freeze the truffles for at least 30 minutes before dipping. The longer they freeze, the easier it will be to dip them.

FOR THE COATING

In a microwave-safe bowl, combine the white chocolate chips and shortening. Microwave in 30-second increments, stirring each time to prevent the chocolate from seizing. I suggest setting the microwave at 50 percent power to prevent the chocolate from burning. Repeat until the chocolate is melted. Whisk the chocolate until it is smooth enough to be easily drizzled. If the chocolate is too thick, you can add additional shortening, 1 tablespoon (14 g) at a time. Allow the white chocolate to cool. Zest the lime into the chocolate and stir to combine. Remove the rolled truffles from the freezer in small batches; it helps keep them from getting too soft. Stick a toothpick in the top of a truffle and swirl it in the chocolate. Tap the truffle on the side of the bowl to remove any excess chocolate. Place it on a piece of parchment paper and use another toothpick to help release the truffle. Sprinkle a little bit of graham cracker crumbs over the top while the chocolate is still warm. Repeat until all of the truffles are covered with chocolate coating and crumbs. Refrigerate the truffles to help the chocolate set more quickly.

chocolate glazed
MARSHMALLOW TREAT DONUTS

I happen to love this recipe because everyone loves Rice Krispies Treats. This is just a super fun way to serve them. Plus sprinkles. I love sprinkles. Imagine serving these at your child's birthday party with a toppings bar that includes your choice of glazes and candy toppings. Oh, my heart just flutters with excitement. If you don't have a donut pan, try making them in a cupcake pan instead!

YIELD: 12 DONUTS

FOR THE TREATS

30 marshmallows, standard size

1 tbsp (14 g) unsalted butter

5 cups (107 g) rice cereal such as Rice Krispies

FOR THE GLAZE

¼ cup (45 g) milk chocolate chips

3 to 4 tbsp (45 to 60 ml) heavy whipping cream, divided

1 cup (130 g) powdered sugar

1 tbsp (15 ml) corn syrup

1 tsp vanilla extract

Sprinkles for garnish

FOR THE TREATS

In a medium-size saucepan, combine the marshmallows and butter. Cook over medium heat and stir until they're completely melted. In a large bowl, add the cereal, pour the melted marshmallows over the cereal, and mix until combined. It will help if you spray t spatula with cooking spray. This will prevent the marshmallows from sticking to it. Allov the marshmallow treat mixture to sit for 5 minutes to cool.

Spray the base of a 6-cavity donut pan with cooking spray. Divide the mixture into 12 donuts. Take a handful of the marshmallow treat mixture and press it into a cavity of the donut pan. Again, it will help if you spray your hand with cooking spray. Repeat until all of the cavities are filled. If you have only 1 pan, allow the first batch to sit for 10 minutes before removing. It's best to let the donuts sit for at least 30 minutes before dipping. That allows the marshmallow to firm up.

FOR THE GLAZE

In a microwave-safe bowl, combine the milk chocolate chips with 1 tablespoon (15 ml) of heavy whipping cream. Microwave for 30 to 45 seconds until the chocolate starts to melt, and stir until it's completely smooth. In the same bowl, add the powdered sugar, corn syrup, vanilla extract, and 2 more tablespoons (30 ml) of heavy whipping cream. Slowly stir together until glaze is completely smooth. If the glaze is still too thick, add the remaining 1 tablespoon (15 ml) of heavy whipping cream and whisk until it's combined. Th glaze should be somewhat thick and not a pourable consistency. Dip the top of each donu in the glaze, tap off any excess glaze and garnish with sprinkles or your favorite candy.

(seven)

puddings and parfaits

Parfaits are underrated. Single-serving layered desserts are perfect for parties, dessert tables or an intimate dinner at home. This chapter covers a variety of parfaits made with both mousse and pudding. There are classic flavors such as coconut cream pie and more modern recipes such as Chocolate Stout Dirt Pudding (page 186). All pudding recipes are made from scratch, even my Cake Batter Cream Pie Parfaits (page 189). If you choose to do so, you can substitute my homemade chocolate pudding with a store-bought mix, but you have to try my chocolate pudding in order to know how much more you will like it.

banana split
SUNDAE PARFAITS

Don't be intimidated by the list of ingredients in this dessert. Once you take the first bite, you'll understand. The mousse is prepared with a banana, cream cheese and marshmallow crème. You might not typically put those flavors together but once combined with the remaining ingredients, the filling will remind you of a banana split crossed with a s'more. The most important step is to allow the mousse filling to set in the refrigerator prior to serving. After doing so, the light and airy mousse can be transferred with an ice cream scoop into the parfait cups and layered with banana split toppings to create a truly unique dessert experience. The best thing about a banana split is that you can make it your own. I've suggested some awesome toppings below, but feel free to substitute with your favorites.

YIELD: 4 PARFAITS

R THE FILLING

cups (355 ml) heavy whipping cream

p (130 g) powdered sugar

z (113 g) cream cheese, softened

edium banana, mashed

z (113 g) marshmallow crème

up (22 g) graham cracker crumbs

sp (34 g) chopped chocolate bar

R THE TOPPING

elgian waffle crisps or waffle cones

edium bananas

p (151 g) strawberries

sp (7 g) sprinkles

araschino cherries

sp (30 ml) hot fudge or caramel sauce

FOR THE FILLING

Prepare the whipped cream by placing the mixing bowl and whisk attachment in the freezer for 5 to 10 minutes to chill. Pour the heavy whipping cream into the chilled bowl and use an electric mixer to beat the heavy cream on medium-high speed until the cream gets bubbly. Slowly add the powdered sugar and continue beating on high speed until stiff peaks form. Set the whipped cream aside. Measure out 1 cup (75 g) of the prepared whipped cream and save it for the parfait topping.

Beat the cream cheese on medium-high speed for 2 to 3 minutes until the cream cheese is smooth and free of lumps. Scrape down the sides of the bowl occasionally. In a small bowl, mash 1 banana into small pieces. Add the mashed banana and beat until it's well mixed into the cream cheese. Spoon in the marshmallow crème and mix it on medium speed until all of the ingredients are well combined, scraping down the sides of the bowl as needed. Finally, add the graham cracker crumbs and the chopped chocolate pieces, and continue to mix until all of the ingredients are well combined. Fold the prepared whipped cream into the cream cheese mixture; the mousse will be thin. Pour the mixture into a container, cover and refrigerate for at least 2 hours to stiffen the mousse.

TO PREPARE THE PARFAITS

Take 4 waffle crisps and crush them into smaller pieces. Divide them evenly among the 4 parfait cups. Use an ice cream scoop to fill the parfait cups with the mousse. To top your parfait, add one waffle crisp to each cup. Add toppings such as sliced bananas, chopped strawberries and sprinkles. Finish by adding the reserved whipped cream and cherries, and drizzle with hot fudge or caramel sauce.

chocolate stout DIRT PUDDING

When I was a kid, my dad's mother would always make a pan of her dirt for our holiday parties. It's a fairly effortless dessert that combines pudding with whipped cream and chocolate sandwich cookies. Sounds easy, right? Well this is an adult twist of my grandma's dirt. It is a homemade chocolate pudding infused with chocolate stout. The filling is so good that you don't even need the cookies, but then it wouldn't be dirt, right? I don't see my grandmother very often, but when I got the chance to visit her recently, we talked about her dirt recipe. I told her I wanted to include a recipe like that in my book. She said, "oh yeah, that's a good one!" This one is for you, Nana!

YIELD: 8 SERVINGS

2 large egg yolks, slightly beaten

3 tbsp (23 g) all-purpose flour

⅓ cup (64 g) granulated sugar

Dash of salt

¾ cup (177 ml) milk

¾ cup (177 ml) chocolate stout

½ tsp vanilla extract

4 oz (113 g) dark chocolate chips

1 ¼ cups (296 ml) heavy whipping cream

¾ cup (98 g) powdered sugar

1 (14-oz [405-g]) package chocolate sandwich cookies (I use Oreos)

½ cup (118 ml) hot fudge sauce

Measure out all of the ingredients for the filling prior to starting. Place the egg yolks in a separate bowl. In a medium-size saucepan, add the flour, sugar and salt and whisk to combine. Add the milk, chocolate stout and vanilla extract. Heat the mixture on the stove top over medium-low heat. Whisk constantly to dissolve the dry ingredients into the milk mixture. Once the mixture is warm (but not boiling), pour about ¼ cup (59 ml) of it into the bowl with the egg yolks and whisk vigorously to temper the egg yolks. Immediately pour the egg yolks into the saucepan and continue whisking over medium-low heat to prevent the eggs from cooking. Whisk until the pudding starts to thicken. Add the chocolate chips to the saucepan and whisk until they're completely melted, and then remove the saucepan from the heat.

Immediately strain the pudding through a fine sieve into a medium-size bowl. This step is optional, but it will help catch any lumps of ingredients that did not get blended. Immediately cover the top of the pudding with clear plastic wrap (directly on the surface of the pudding) and poke a few holes with a toothpick. Allow it to cool on the counter for at least 1 hour before refrigerating. Refrigerate for 2 to 3 hours until the pudding has cooled and is firm.

Once the pudding is firm, prepare the whipped cream. Place the mixing bowl and whisk attachment in the freezer for 5 to 10 minutes to chill. Pour the heavy whipping cream into the chilled bowl and use an electric mixer to beat the heavy cream on medium-high speed until the cream gets bubbly. Slowly add the powdered sugar and continue beating on high speed until stiff peaks form. Slowly add the pudding into the whipped cream, folding and stirring together until all of the ingredients are combined to create a mousse.

TO ASSEMBLE THE DESSERT

Crush the cookies in a plastic bag using a rolling pin or similar object to break the cookies into pieces. In a 9-inch (23-cm) square pan, pour ⅔ of the cookie crumbs into the bottom of the pan. Pour the mousse over the top of the cookie crumbs and spread evenly. Top with the remaining crushed cookies. Heat the hot fudge sauce according to instructions on the jar. Drizzle the hot fudge over the top of the crushed cookies. Refrigerate for another 2 to 4 hours before serving to allow the cookies to soften and the mousse to set and firm.

cake batter
CREAM PIE PARFAITS

When I was developing the concept for this cookbook, a homemade cake batter pudding was something I really wanted to create. I am so happy with the results. For this recipe, I use dry cake mix instead of flour as the thickening agent for the pudding. After the pudding sets, it's mixed with a homemade whipped cream to lighten up the texture. This parfait is layered with crushed vanilla cookies and topped with whipped cream.

YIELD: 4 TO 6 PARFAITS

R THE PUDDING
rge egg yolks, slightly beaten

p gelatin

sp (15 ml) cold water

sp (16 g) vanilla cake mix, dry

up (48 g) granulated sugar

sh of salt

cups (592 ml) heavy whipping cream, ded

up (98 g) powdered sugar

R THE TOPPING AND LAYERS
up (177 ml) heavy whipping cream

up (65 g) powdered sugar

cups (112 g) vanilla sandwich cookie mbs (I use Golden Oreos)

sp (7 g) sprinkles

FOR THE PUDDING

Measure out all of the ingredients for the pudding prior to starting. Place the egg yolks in a separate bowl. In a medium-size saucepan, pour the gelatin over cold water and let it sit for 2 minutes. Turn the heat on medium-low and allow the gelatin to turn back to liquid. Quickly add the vanilla cake mix, granulated sugar, salt and 1 ¼ cups (296 ml) of heavy whipping cream. Whisk constantly to dissolve the dry ingredients in the mixture.

Once the mixture is warm (but not boiling), pour about ¼ cup (59 ml) of it into the bowl with the egg yolks and whisk vigorously to temper the egg yolks. Immediately pour the egg yolks into the saucepan and continue whisking over medium-low heat to prevent the eggs from cooking. Whisk until the pudding starts to thicken and then remove it from the heat; it will happen very quickly.

Immediately strain the pudding through a fine sieve into a medium-size bowl. This step is optional, but it will help catch any lumps of ingredients that did not get blended. Immediately cover the top of the pudding with clear plastic wrap (directly on the surface of the pudding) and poke a few holes with a toothpick. Allow it to cool on the counter for at least 1 hour before refrigerating. Refrigerate for 2 to 3 hours until the pudding has cooled and is firm.

Once the pudding has firmed, prepare the whipped cream. Place the mixing bowl and whisk attachment in the freezer for 5 to 10 minutes to chill. Pour remaining 1 ¼ cups (296 ml) of heavy whipping cream into the chilled bowl and use an electric mixer to beat the heavy cream on medium-high speed until the cream gets bubbly. Slowly add the powdered sugar and continue beating on high speed until stiff peaks form. Fold the whipped cream into the pudding until it's smooth.

FOR THE TOPPING AND LAYERS

Combine the whipping cream and powdered sugar as described above to prepare a second batch of whipped cream.

Before measuring, grind the cookies into fine crumbs using a food processor or blender. To assemble your parfaits, each will have 2 layers of crumbs, 2 layers of mousse and will be topped with whipped cream. The parfait cups can be easily filled with the mousse if you use a large piping bag. Start with a layer of crumbs, and then pipe on a layer of mousse, followed by another layer of crumbs and a top layer of mousse. Finish each parfait with a swirl of whipped topping and some sprinkles. The parfaits must be refrigerated until served.

mudslide PARFAITS

For this recipe, I have taken my homemade chocolate pudding and spiked it with coffee liqueur to add a whole new level of flavor. These parfaits are layered with a chocolate cookie crust, the spiked pudding and an Irish cream whipped cream. Now if you don't have both coffee liqueur and Irish cream liqueur on hand, you can use just one or the other, but the combination of both is what makes this parfait come to life.

YIELD: 4 PARFAITS

FOR THE FILLING

2 large egg yolks, slightly beaten

3 tbsp (23 g) all-purpose flour

⅓ cup (64 g) granulated sugar

Dash of salt

¾ cup (177 ml) milk

¾ cup (177 ml) coffee liqueur such as Kahlua

1 tsp vanilla extract

4 oz (113 g) dark chocolate chips

FOR THE TOPPING

¾ cup (177 ml) heavy whipping cream

1 tbsp (15 ml) Irish cream such as Bailey's Irish Cream

¼ cup (33 g) powdered sugar

½ cup (118 ml) hot fudge sauce

¾ cup (67 g) chocolate sandwich cookie crumbs (I use Oreos)

Sprinkles for garnish (optional)

FOR THE FILLING

Measure out all of the ingredients for the filling prior to starting. Place the egg yolks in a separate bowl. In a medium-size saucepan, add the flour, sugar and salt, and whisk to combine. Add the milk, coffee liqueur and vanilla extract. Heat the mixture on the stove top over medium-low heat. Whisk constantly to dissolve the dry ingredients into the milk mixtu Once the mixture is warm (but not boiling), pour about ¼ cup (59 ml) of it into the bowl wi the egg yolks and whisk vigorously to temper the egg yolks. Immediately pour the egg yol into the saucepan and continue whisking over medium-low heat to prevent the eggs from cooking. Whisk until the pudding starts to thicken. Add the chocolate chips to the mixture and whisk until they're completely melted. Remove it from the heat as the pudding starts to thicken; it will happen pretty quickly.

Immediately strain the pudding through a fine sieve into a medium-size bowl. This step is optional, but it will help catch any lumps of ingredients that did not get blended. Immediate cover the top of the pudding (directly on the pudding surface) with clear plastic wrap, and poke a few holes with a toothpick. Allow the pudding to cool on the counter for at least 1 h before refrigerating. Refrigerate for 2 to 3 hours until the pudding has cooled and is firm.

FOR THE TOPPING

The whipped topping can be prepared in advance or you can prepare it right before serving Place the mixing bowl and whisk attachment in the freezer for 5 to 10 minutes to chill. Pour t heavy whipping cream into the chilled bowl and use an electric mixer to beat the heavy crea on medium-high speed until the cream gets bubbly. Add the Irish cream and the powdered sugar, and continue beating on high speed until stiff peaks form. This will be slightly less stiff than a traditional whipped cream due to the addition of the liqueur.

TO ASSEMBLE THE PARFAITS

Heat the hot fudge sauce according to the instructions on the jar. Pick up your parfait glass and turn it sideways. Use a spoonful of hot fudge and slowly drizzle it on the inside edges of the glass, gently rotating the glass as you go. Repeat with remaining glasses. Before measuring, crush the cookies in a plastic bag using a rolling pin or similar object to break tl cookies into pieces, or grind the cookies into fine crumbs using a food processor or blende Pour 2 to 3 tablespoons (11 to 17 g) of cookie crumbs in the bottom of each glass.

Pour the pudding into a piping bag or similar bag to fill the glasses with pudding, dividin evenly between each glass. Of course, you can also use a spoon instead. Use a knife or spoon to spread the pudding out to the edges. Pipe the Irish cream whipped topping ont the pudding, dividing evenly among the glasses. Serve immediately or keep refrigerated until ready to serve. Garnish with sprinkles or additional hot fudge sauce.

coconut cream pie PARFAITS

If you had told me when I was younger that I would come to love coconut desserts as an adult, I probably wouldn't have believed you. My sister has always been the coconut lover of the family, and whenever I turned my nose up at a coconut dessert, she just said, "oh well, more for me." At some point things changed, and now I am not sure I could ever pass up a coconut cream pie. The pudding is rich and silky. It's made with milk and sweetened condensed milk and a hint of coconut extract. With the combination of the vanilla wafer cookie crust, the coconut pudding and fresh whipped cream, my Coconut Cream Pie Parfaits will satisfy any coconut cravings.

YIELD: 4 PARFAITS

R THE PUDDING

rge egg yolks, slightly beaten

up (31 g) all-purpose flour

up (128 g) granulated sugar

ups (473 ml) milk

4-oz [316-g]) can sweetened
densed milk

o coconut extract

R THE TOPPING

p (237 ml) heavy whipping cream

up (65 g) powdered sugar

R THE CRUST

p (90 g) vanilla wafer crumbs (I use
a wafers)

osp (43 g) unsalted butter

eetened flaked coconut for garnish

FOR THE PUDDING

Measure out all of the ingredients for the pudding prior to starting. Place the egg yolks in a separate bowl. In a medium-size saucepan, add the flour and sugar, and whisk to combine. Add the milk, sweetened condensed milk and coconut extract. Heat the mixture on the stove top over medium-low heat. Whisk constantly to dissolve the dry ingredients. Once the mixture is warm (but not boiling), pour about ¼ cup (59 ml) of it into the bowl with the egg yolks and whisk vigorously to temper the egg yolks. Immediately pour the egg yolks into the saucepan and continue whisking over medium-low heat to prevent the eggs from cooking. Whisk until the pudding starts to thicken and then remove it from the heat; it will happen pretty quickly.

Immediately strain the pudding through a fine sieve into a medium-size bowl. This step is optional, but it will help catch any lumps of ingredients that did not get blended. Immediately cover the top of the pudding (directly on the pudding surface) with clear plastic wrap, and poke a couple holes with a toothpick. Allow to cool on the counter for at least 1 hour before refrigerating. Refrigerate for 4 to 6 hours until the pudding has cooled and is firm.

FOR THE TOPPING

Place the mixing bowl and whisk attachment in the freezer for 5 to 10 minutes to chill. Pour the heavy whipping cream into the chilled bowl and use an electric mixer to beat the heavy cream on medium-high speed until the cream gets bubbly. Slowly add the powdered sugar and continue beating on high speed until stiff peaks form. You will be dividing the whipped cream between 4 parfait cups.

FOR THE CRUST

Before measuring, use a food processor or blender to grind the wafer cookies into fine crumbs. In a microwave-safe bowl, combine the crumbs with butter and melt in the microwave for 30 to 60 seconds, stirring occasionally.

TO ASSEMBLE THE DESSERT

Divide the ingredients equally among the parfaits. Add about 3 tablespoons (17 g) of cookie crumbs to the bottom of each cup and gently press down with a spoon. Fill each cup with the coconut pudding and top with whipped cream. Sprinkle with flaked coconut and refrigerate before serving.

peach and maple
CREAM PARFAITS

There are few things that Vermont is known for and maple syrup is one of them. I wanted to be sure to include a maple syrup recipe in my book, and maple custard seemed like the perfect solution. I don't get back to Vermont very often, and when I do, I try to set aside time to eat all of my favorite things. Maple custard ice cream is a summer favorite, and it can be hard to come by. This inspired me to make these parfaits, and I've decided to top them with sliced peaches. These parfaits are a labor of love. I suggest you read through the entire recipe before starting, and allow yourself plenty of time for these to set. Don't be intimidated by the steps; they just take a little bit of patience.

YIELD: 6 PARFAITS

FOR THE CUSTARD

2 large egg yolks, slightly beaten

4 tbsp (31 g) all-purpose flour

¼ cup (48 g) granulated sugar

Dash of salt

2 ¾ cups (651 ml) heavy whipping cream, divided

3 tbsp (44 ml) maple syrup

¾ cup (98 g) powdered sugar

FOR THE PEACHES

6 medium peaches, washed and sliced

1 tbsp (8 g) cinnamon

2 tbsp (28 g) light brown sugar

3 tbsp (44 ml) maple syrup

FOR THE TOPPING

1 ¼ cups (296 ml) heavy whipping cream

¾ cup (98 g) powdered sugar

¼ tsp cinnamon for garnish (optional)

FOR THE CUSTARD

Measure out all of the ingredients for the custard prior to starting. Place the egg yolks in a separate bowl. In a medium-size saucepan, add the flour, granulated sugar and salt and whisk to combine. Add 1 ½ cups (355 ml) of heavy whipping cream and the maple syrup. Heat the mixture on the stove top over medium-low heat. Whisk constantly to dissolve the dry the ingredients into the cream mixture. Once the mixture is warm (but not boiling), pour about ¼ cup (59 ml) of the cream mixture into the egg yolks and whisk vigorously to temper. Immediately pour the egg yolks into the saucepan and continue whisking over medium-low heat to prevent the eggs from cooking. Whisk until the custard starts to thicken. Once the mixture is thick and bubbly, remove it from the heat.

Immediately strain the custard through a fine sieve into a medium-size bowl. This step is optional, but it will help catch any lumps of ingredients that did not get blended. Immediately cover the top of the custard with clear plastic wrap (directly on the surface of custard) and poke a few holes with a toothpick. Allow the custard to cool for 30 minutes at room temperature, and then refrigerate it for 2 hours until the custard is cold.

After 2 hours, prepare the whipped cream to be mixed into the custard. Place the mixing bowl and whisk attachment in the freezer for 5 to 10 minutes to chill. Pour the remaining 1 ¼ cups (296 ml) of heavy whipping cream into the chilled bowl and use an electric mixer to beat the heavy cream on medium-high speed until the cream gets bubbly. Slowly add the powdered sugar and continue beating on high speed until stiff peaks form. Fold the whipped cream into your custard.

At this point, the custard will be thin again. Pour the custard into a large plastic bag and cut off one of the bottom corners to make a basic piping bag. Line up the parfait cups and divide the custard among the cups, filling them about ¾ full. Place the parfait cups the refrigerator for 3 hours until the custard is firm.

(continue

FOR THE PEACHES

While the custard is setting, prepare the peaches. I left my peaches as whole slices, but you could certainly dice them. You do not need to peel the peaches. In a large bowl, toss the peaches together with cinnamon, brown sugar and maple syrup. Pour them into a large skillet. Cook the peaches over medium heat until they're soft but not mushy. Allow the peaches to cool to room temperature and refrigerate until ready to serve.

Once the individual custards are set, divide the peaches among each parfait and prepare the whipped cream topping.

FOR THE TOPPING

Combine the whipping cream and powdered sugar as described previously to prepare a second batch of whipped cream. Divide the whipped cream among the parfait cups. Sprinkle the top of each with a touch of cinnamon (optional). Keep refrigerated until ready to serve.

eggnog gingerbread
PUDDING PARFAITS

I find that people have a love-hate relationship with eggnog. Personally, I'm a fan. For these parfaits, I've used eggnog for the homemade pudding instead of milk or heavy whipping cream. This means this pudding is purely eggnog based, plus it's flavored with a hint of nutmeg. These eggnog parfaits are also jazzed up with a gingersnap cookie crust, but if you don't love gingersnaps, try this with graham crackers instead. Is anyone else hoarding all the eggnog?

YIELD: 4 PARFAITS

FOR THE FILLING

large egg yolks, slightly beaten

tbsp (23 g) all-purpose flour

cup (64g) granulated sugar

dash of salt

tsp nutmeg, ground

cups (355 ml) eggnog

tsp vanilla extract

cup (161 g) gingersnap cookie crumbs

tbsp (43 g) unsalted butter

FOR THE TOPPING

cup (237 ml) heavy whipping cream

cup (65 g) powdered sugar

FOR THE FILLING

Measure out all of the ingredients for the filling prior to starting. Place the egg yolks in a separate bowl. In a medium-size saucepan, add the flour, sugar, salt and nutmeg, and whisk to combine. Add the eggnog and vanilla extract. Heat the mixture on the stove top over medium-low heat. Whisk constantly to dissolve the dry ingredients into the eggnog mixture. Once the mixture is warm (but not boiling), pour about ¼ cup (59 ml) of it into the bowl with the egg yolks and whisk vigorously to temper the egg yolks. Immediately pour the egg yolks into the saucepan and continue whisking over medium-low heat to prevent the eggs from cooking. Whisk until the pudding starts to bubble and thicken, and then remove it from the heat.

Immediately strain the pudding through a fine sieve into a medium-size bowl. This step is optional, but it will help catch any lumps of ingredients that did not get blended. Immediately cover the top of the pudding with clear plastic wrap (directly on the pudding surface) and poke a few holes with a toothpick. Allow the pudding to cool for 30 minutes at room temperature, and then refrigerate for 3 to 4 hours until it has cooled and is firm.

Before measuring, use a food processor to grind the gingersnaps into fine crumbs. In a microwave-safe bowl, microwave the butter for 45 to 60 seconds until melted. In a separate medium-size bowl, pour the melted butter over the gingersnap crumbs and stir until the crumbs are well coated.

TO ASSEMBLE THE DESSERT

Divide the ingredients equally among the parfait cups. You will have 2 layers of crumbs and 2 layers of pudding in each parfait. Add about 1 to 2 tablespoons (5 to 11 g) of crumbs to the bottom of each cup and gently press down with a spoon. Add a thin pudding layer on top of the crust followed by another 1 tablespoon (5 g) of gingersnap crumbs and top with the remaining pudding.

(continued)

eggnog gingerbread
PUDDING PARFAITS (CONT.)

FOR THE TOPPING

Place the mixing bowl and whisk attachment in the freezer for 5 to 10 minutes to chill. Pour the heavy whipping cream into the chilled bowl and use an electric mixer to beat the heavy cream on medium-high speed until the cream gets bubbly. Slowly add the powdered sugar and continue beating at a high speed until stiff peaks form. Divide the whipped cream among the 4 parfait cups. Sprinkle the top with any leftover gingersnap crumbs. The parfaits must be refrigerated until served.

mississippi mud pie PARFAITS

My simple Mississippi Mud Pie Parfaits have plenty of layers to go around. The chocolate pudding sits on top of a thick cookie crust. You have, of course, crushed pecans, whipped cream and chocolate sauce drizzled on top. If there's one thing to know about a Mississippi Mud Pie dessert, is that it is loaded with chocolate, and there is no shortage of chocolate in these parfaits.

YIELD: 4 PARFAITS

FOR THE FILLING

2 large egg yolks, slightly beaten

3 tbsp (23 g) all-purpose flour

⅓ cup (64 g) granulated sugar

Dash of salt

1 ½ cups (355 ml) milk

½ tsp vanilla extract

4 oz (113 g) dark chocolate chips

FOR THE TOPPING AND LAYERS

¾ cup (177 ml) heavy whipping cream

¼ cup (33 g) powdered sugar

¾ cup (67 g) chocolate sandwich cookie crumbs (I use Oreos)

2 tbsp (29 g) unsalted butter

¼ cup (40 g) crushed pecans

2 tbsp (30 ml) hot fudge sauce

FOR THE FILLING

Measure out all of the ingredients for the filling prior to starting. Place the egg yolks in a separate bowl. In a medium-size saucepan, add the flour, sugar and salt, and whisk to combine. Add the milk and vanilla extract. Heat the mixture on the stove top over medium-low heat. Whisk constantly to dissolve the dry ingredients into the milk mixture. Once the mixture is warm (but not boiling), pour about ¼ cup (59 ml) of it into the bowl with the egg yolks and whisk vigorously to temper the egg yolks. Immediately pour the egg yolks into the saucepan and continue whisking over medium-low heat to prevent the eggs from cooking. Whisk until the pudding starts to thicken. Add the chocolate chips to the mixture and whisk until they're completely melted. Remove it from the heat as the pudding continues to thicken; it will happen pretty quickly.

Immediately strain the pudding through a fine sieve into a medium-size bowl. This step is optional, but it will help catch any lumps of ingredients that did not get blended. Immediately cover the top of the pudding with clear plastic wrap (directly on the pudding surface) and poke a few holes with a toothpick. Allow the pudding to cool on the counter for at least 1 hour before refrigerating. Refrigerate for 2 to 3 hours until the pudding has cooled and is firm.

FOR THE TOPPING AND LAYERS

The whipped cream should be prepared right before serving for best results. Place the mixing bowl and whisk attachment in the freezer for 5 to 10 minutes to chill. Pour the heavy whipping cream into the chilled bowl and use an electric mixer to beat the heavy cream on medium-high speed until the cream gets bubbly. Slowly add the powdered sugar and continue beating on high speed until stiff peaks form.

Before measuring, grind the cookies into fine crumbs using a food processor or blender. In a microwave-safe bowl, microwave the butter for 45 to 60 seconds until melted. In a separate medium-size bowl, pour the melted butter into the crumbs until there are no dry crumbs left. Spoon 2 to 3 tablespoons (11 to 17 g) of cookie crumbs into the bottom of each parfait cup and gently press down with a spoon.

Pour the pudding into a piping bag or similar bag and use it to fill the cups with pudding, dividing evenly among each cup. Of course, you can also use a spoon instead. Use a knife or spoon to spread the pudding out to the edges. Sprinkle with crushed pecans and top with whipped cream. Heat the hot fudge sauce according to the instruction on the jar and drizzle it over the top of the whipped cream. Serve these immediately or refrigerate until ready to serve.

strawberries and cream
PARFAITS

This is perhaps the easiest parfait to prepare, but don't underestimate how much you will love this dessert. You can make and enjoy this dessert as soon as you bring home some fresh strawberries. I've always loved strawberries and whipped cream, which is what this dessert is all about. I've taken the whipped cream to the next level by adding some cream cheese, giving you a hint of cheesecake filling to go along with your strawberries.

YIELD: 4 LARGE OR 6 SMALL PARFAITS

R THE CRUST

ups (180 g) graham cracker crumbs

osp (86 g) unsalted butter

R THE FILLING

z (227 g) cream cheese, softened

cups (296 ml) heavy whipping cream

up (65 g) powdered sugar

z (113 g) strawberries, chopped

FOR THE CRUST

Before measuring, grind the graham crackers into fine crumbs using a food processor or blender. In a microwave-safe bowl, microwave the butter for 45 to 60 seconds until melted. In a separate medium-size bowl, pour the melted butter into the crumbs until there are no dry crumbs left. Divide the graham cracker crumbs among the parfait cups.

FOR THE FILLING

Beat the softened cream cheese with a whisk attachment on medium-high speed for 2 to 3 minutes until it's light and fluffy, and then scrape the sides of the bowl. Reduce the mixer speed to low and slowly add the heavy whipping cream about ¼ cup (59 ml) at a time, allowing the cream cheese to turn to a liquid consistency. Once all of the whipping cream has been added, increase the speed to high until the mixture becomes bubbly. Then slowly add the powdered sugar and continue beating until stiff peaks form. Reserve ½ cup (38 g) of the filling for garnish.

Pour the filling into a piping bag. Pipe the filling into the parfaits cups, leaving about ¾ of the cup to add a garnish. Of course, you can also use a spoon to fill the cups instead. Sprinkle the chopped strawberries over the filling and garnish with a small swirl of the reserved filling.

(eight)

helpful tips and tools

In this section you will find helpful tips for various tasks from preparing your crusts to choosing ingredients. You will also find step-by-step instructions and photos for using various tools necessary for successful baking, such as preparing your pans, dipping your candies and layering your favorite desserts.

I'll start by saying that you'll want to read through an entire recipe before starting. Most no-bake refrigerated desserts need time to prepare and set in the refrigerator before serving. They may need anywhere from 4 to 8 hours to prepare. One great thing is that some recipes can usually be prepared ahead of time. That way you won't have to worry about dessert as you scramble to prepare for a dinner party with friends!

CHOOSING THE RIGHT CRUST

You will notice I use a variety of different types of crusts. You have classic crusts that use chocolate sandwich cookies (I use Oreos) and graham crackers, and less traditional crusts that call for Ritz crackers or potato chips. There is something for everyone, and it's helpful to know what your options are.

Most crusts start with finely ground crumbs and are mixed with a binding agent such as butter, corn syrup or honey. I prefer to use butter. Occasionally, you'll notice that I add brown sugar or spices such as cinnamon to a crust to give it an extra spike in flavor.

If you are unsure whether or not you added enough butter to your crust, try pressing it into the pan. If the crust doesn't hold together or you have a hard time pressing it up on the sides of your pan, pour it back into your mixing bowl and add some additional melted butter. Mix it well.

COOKIES AND CRACKERS

My most common type of cookie crust uses chocolate sandwich cookies (I use Oreos). I never bother to take the filling out of the Oreos, that's too much work! I throw the whole Oreo in my food processor and grind it up. Oreos come in different varieties, most of which I have used for my crusts. Other varieties include Golden Oreos, or vanilla sandwich cookie; Lemon Oreos and Birthday Cake Oreos. Oreos come in different size packages. I consider the standard size to be 14 ounces (405 g), which will satisfy a majority of the recipes in this cookbook. A full package of Oreos is about 3 ½ cups (315 g) of crumbs. Some recipes call for less.

A package of Oreos has 36 cookies. If you grind 12 Oreos you will get about 1 ¼ cups (112 g) of crumbs. To get 2 ¼ to 2 ½ cups (202 to 225 g), you will need 24 to 28 Oreos.

Shortbread cookies make a wonderful crust as well. These cookies tend to have a higher butter content, which means you will need less melted butter to bind the crust. You usually will need to use half as much butter with shortbread cookies as you would use for an Oreo-type crust. Feel free to try different varieties of shortbread cookies such as lemon or chocolate if the filling lends itself to those flavors.

Vanilla wafers such as Nilla wafers are a great alternative to graham crackers or Golden Oreos. They are a bit lighter in flavor and color and lend themselves nicely to recipes such as my Banana Cream Pudding Cheesecake.

Peanut butter sandwich cookies such as Nutter Butters are quite addicting for me. These work well for peanut butter desserts but also complement other flavors such as chocolate and banana. Consider adding your own twist and swapping out chocolate sandwich cookies or graham crackers for the peanut butter sandwich cookies.

When it comes time to make a holiday treat, I usually turn to gingersnaps. They pair nicely with flavors such as eggnog and pumpkin. Gingerbread is really an acquired taste, so if you are unsure of your audience, you might consider opting for graham crackers instead.

Graham crackers are the most common type of cracker that I use. Graham crackers grind up into nice fine crumbs in the food processor. They are lightly sweetened and often don't compete with the flavor of the filling. I use a few different types of graham crackers in this cookbook, including the standard honey graham crackers. But cinnamon and chocolate graham crackers are good as well. The cinnamon-flavored graham crackers add a wonderful flavor to the crust.

For a salty crust, you might consider a cracker such as Ritz, or potato chips. Each makes a very different crust. A cracker tends to be drier and may require additional butter to bind the crust together. Potato chips, on the other hand, are very greasy and need to be ground up very fine. The amount of butter needed will vary. To best determine this, press the crust together in your hands. If it does not fall apart easily, it should be good to go.

A couple of my recipes call for Belgian waffle crisps. These are thin waffle-like cookies that are lightly sweetened. They are flat cookies, similar to graham crackers but thinner. You can usually find these in the cookie aisle alongside the fancy cookies. You can also find them in specialty food stores. When in doubt, graham crackers are the best substitute.

PERFECT WHIPPED CREAM

You'll notice all but one recipe in my book calls for homemade whipped cream instead of store-bought whipped topping. I use this method because premade whipped topping is not available everywhere in the world. However, in most cases you can substitute a premade whipped topping to help save preparation time. It is also useful for those beautifully piped borders.

The key to a successful whipped cream involves a few simple elements. The first is cold ingredients and utensils. All recipes in my book call for heavy whipping cream, as opposed to heavy cream. Whipping cream contains a higher fat content, which will hold a better shape and produce a thicker whipped cream.

I always recommend placing your mixing bowl and even your whisk in the freezer prior to making whipped cream. It will help keep the cream nice and cold. I also prefer to use a metal mixing bowl because it gets colder than a glass bowl. All that's needed is 5 to 10 minutes in the freezer. It goes without saying that the actual whipping cream needs to be cold as well, so I keep that in the refrigerator until I'm ready to use it.

I always prefer to prepare the whipped cream just prior to serving, unless it needs to be frozen. The reason for this is that I want it to be fresh, and it also holds up best when fresh. For example, I usually want to add borders to the edge of my desserts, which means I need to take the sides off the springform or tart pan. The desserts need to be completely set before doing so. Then, after removing the sides, I can prepare and apply fresh whipped cream. However, if you do need to make the whipped cream the night before serving, I suggest piping it onto your dessert at that time as opposed to leaving it in a bowl overnight.

I also never use less than ¾ cup (177 ml) or more than 1 ¾ cups (414 ml) of heavy whipping cream at one time because it can be more difficult for the whipped cream to form properly when using less or more than these amounts. I always err on the side of making more whipped cream than I'll actually need. Plus, I love to eat it with a spoon, so I get all of the leftovers!

Whipped cream needs to be whipped at a high speed. I always start on medium-high, which is speed 6 on my stand mixer. Once the whipped cream is bubbly and starts to thicken, add the powdered sugar slowly; otherwise, you will get a powdered sugar shower, and no one likes to clean that up.

The most important part of making a stable whipped cream is adding something to help stiffen it up. My preferred stabilizer is powdered sugar. You will notice that I tend to use a lot of powdered sugar to make my whipped cream nice and stiff, which is perfect for piping! Below is a table of helpful measurements that will ensure a nice, stiff whipped cream. This is a general guide, and, as always, there are exceptions to my rules.

¾ cup (177 ml) heavy whipping cream plus ¼ cup (33 g) powdered sugar makes 7 ¼ ounces (205 g), or about 2 cups (150 g) prepared.

1 cup (237 ml) heavy whipping cream plus ½ cup (65 g) powdered sugar makes 10 ounces (284 g), or about 2 ¼ cups (168 g) prepared.

1 ¼ cups (296 ml) heavy whipping cream plus ½ cup and 2 tablespoons (114 g) powdered sugar makes 12 ounces (314 g), or about 2 ¾ cups (207 g) prepared.

1 ½ cups (355 ml) heavy whipping cream plus ¾ cup (98 g) powdered sugar makes 14 ounces (397 g), or about 3 ½ cups (263 g) prepared.

1 ¾ cups (414 ml) heavy whipping cream plus 1 cup (130 g) powdered sugar makes about 16 ounces (454 g), or about 4 cups (300 g) prepared.

CHOOSING A GARNISH

After you have gone through all of the necessary steps to prepare your gorgeous dessert, you will need to consider the finishing touches. In my recipes, I suggest lots of different garnishes such as hot fudge, caramel, berries, sprinkles, crushed cookies or a sprinkle of cinnamon. It's always nice to sprinkle the tops of the whipped cream with a little bit of the cookies you used in the crust, a zest of fruit or some chocolate shavings.

You can make the chocolate shavings in a couple of ways. You can hold a chocolate bar in your hand and drag a vegetable peeler along the edge or you can use a sharp knife to finely shave along the edge of the chocolate bar.

The one garnish I use most often is hot fudge sauce. Hot fudge sauce makes the most perfect topping to drizzle over slices of cheesecake, a parfait or a tart. It's much easier to prepare than a ganache, and one jar goes a long way. In addition to drizzling it over a finished dessert, I love to drizzle the sauce over the plate for a little dessert pizzazz! You can find this common ingredient near the ice cream section in the store. I prefer brands such as Hershey's, Smuckers or Ghirardelli.

PREPARING YOUR SPRINGFORM PAN

You'll notice that a few of my recipes include specific directions to prepare the springform pans. First, I line the bottom with aluminum foil and wrap it around the sides tightly. This helps in a number of ways. For one thing, I won't have to scrub the base to clean all the crumbs out, but that's just a bonus. Occasionally, I will line the bottom with a large piece of parchment paper instead of foil. The parchment paper also allows for a swift and easy transfer to a cake plate.

It helps to wipe the sides of the springform pan with a nonstick cooking spray. To do this, I spray a paper towel and wipe the inside edges. This helps prevent the crust from sticking to the sides of the pan. There is nothing worse than releasing the springform edge and having your crust fall apart because it sticks to the sides of the pan.

When it's time to remove a cheesecake from the pan, I unwrap the foil from the bottom and quickly lift the foil with the cake from the pan. I can then transfer the cheesecake to a cake stand or serving tray. One helpful tool I have is a cake lifter. It's basically a large square spatula that can easily be slid underneath a cake. If this step makes you nervous, try freezing your cheesecake for 30 minutes before attempting to do this.

BUILDING A LAYERED DESSERT

There are a few helpful things you can do to ensure success when cutting and serving your layered dessert. First, line the bottom of your pan with parchment paper. This allows you to get underneath the bottom layer without it sticking to the pan.

Another good practice is to lay out the crackers or cookies for the crust in a manner that allows for maximum coverage without breaking too many pieces. You may notice that if you lay the whole graham crackers one way versus the other, you can get more surface area covered. When it's time to fill in the gaps and cracks, cut your crackers to fit. I find it easiest to use a serrated knife and cut the crackers slowly to get a nice clean edge. If your layered dessert is to be frozen, you don't have to worry as much about filling in those cracks because it will naturally bind together once frozen.

If you have layers of fruit or any type of chunky filling, do your best to press it into the soft filling so that any layer on top of it will lay flat.

Spreading that first layer of filling over the bottom layer of crackers can be a little frustrating because there is nothing to hold the crackers in place. Just be patient and use your offset spatula and your fingers to hold the crackers in place as you spread the filling.

Align the graham crackers to best fit the pan. The larger pieces will provide support for the dessert, so lay them out in a way that allows the most whole pieces of crackers. Slice the crackers to fit as need to fill in the smaller gaps.

Spread the filling over the bottom layer of crackers and continue to build your next layer. This time, rotate your crackers in the opposite direction so that it adds stability to the icebox cake.

Continue to build the layers and add your favorite topping. Most icebox cakes take at least 3 hours for the crackers to soften to a cake-like texture.

CANDY DIPPING

Chocolate-dipped treats can be a little intimidating, but if you follow a few simple techniques, you can be successful. Just remember that not everything comes out perfect the first time. Your first decision will be whether you want to use dipping chocolate (Wilton Candy Melts or an almond bark such as Candiquik) or chocolate chips. I have used both and in my opinion, they each have their positives and negatives.

Dipping chocolates are great for homemade candy bars, such as peanut butter cups, chocolate-dipped strawberries and even truffles. They set quickly but are not as creamy as pure chocolate. Dipping chocolates are also available in a variety of colors, which is great if you want to make something such as a cake pop. I do use these from time to time. The exception is when I need white chocolate. I always use a type of almond bark or Candiquik when I need white chocolate.

I prefer a dark chocolate coating, so I like to use high-quality dark chocolate chips or bars. I do find that after they are chilled, the chocolate coating remains a bit softer than you might find with dipping chocolates. So when it comes time to make my Strawberry Margarita Cheesecake Bites or my Mint Chocolate Ice Cream Bites, the dark chocolate coating is ideal. This chocolate must be melted (also referred to as tempered) at a low temperature and in stages. If you are using a microwave, it is best to melt it at 50 percent power and in 30-second increments, stirring each time. The chocolate will not completely melt in the microwave; this only happens once you start to really stir it.

Perhaps the most difficult part is getting the chocolate to the right consistency for dipping. I always add vegetable oil or shortening (such as Crisco) as I melt my chocolate chips or bars to help make it thin enough to dip. Some dipping chocolate might also require the addition of vegetable oil or shortening as well. I start by adding a small amount such as 1 to 2 tablespoons (15 to 30 ml), and continue adding as needed until the chocolate is running off my spoon in a smooth stream. If you add too much, the chocolate can become too oily and thus take longer to set. The chocolate will also need to cool for about 10 minutes. If you dip a truffle when the chocolate is too hot, your chocolate will crack. It is always best to test the first one and wait for it set before dipping a whole bunch. It is such a bummer when you end up with a handful of truffles that are all cracked.

Once your chocolate reaches a smooth consistency, prepare to start dipping. I like to dip truffles that have been previously frozen so they are stiff and do not fall apart when dipping. I also dip in small batches, maybe 5 to 10 at a time. Place your truffle on top of your fork and dip into the chocolate. Use a spoon to pour the chocolate over the top of the truffle. Once it is covered, tap the fork on the sides of the bowl to knock off any excess chocolate. Then run the bottom edge of the fork on the edge of the bowl to knock off excess chocolate from the bottom. Use a toothpick to help nudge the truffle off the fork and onto your silicone mat.

I always place my truffles on a nonstick silicone mat. If one is not available, I suggest parchment paper. These surfaces allow me to easily remove the truffle without breaking the chocolate apart. Never put truffles on a wire rack. Once you lift up a truffle, the bottom will likely stick to the wire rack and your truffle will be ruined. You should ensure the chocolate is completely set before moving truffles. I like to refrigerate them for at least 30 minutes.

BAKING TOOLS AND PANS

This book would not be complete without describing the pots and pans of various shapes and sizes, spatulas, measuring cups and lots and lots of dishes that will be needed. In fact, one of my friends who tested recipes for me asked me if I always washed this many dishes. The answer is yes. During the 6 months of preparing this book, I washed more dishes than I probably will in my entire life. Here is some information about all of my favorite kitchen gadgets and helpful tools.

(continued)

the truffle as smoothly as possible and freeze for at least 30 minutes prior ipping.

Melt and whisk the chocolate until it smoothly runs off your spoon.

ce the frozen truffle on top of your fork and lower it into the ted chocolate.

Lift the truffle out of the chocolate and allow the excess chocolate to drip off the truffle. Gently tap the fork on the side of the bowl and run the bottom of the fork along the edge of the bowl to knock off any excess chocolate.

a toothpick to help transfer the truffle off the fork and onto your one mat.

Drizzle any leftover chocolate over top and put the truffles in the refrigerator to allow the truffles to set.

SPRINGFORM PANS

If there is one pan you should buy to accompany this cookbook, it's a springform pan. A springform pan is typically used for cheesecake. The bottom of the pan can be separated from the sides with a simple spring hinge. Nearly all of the recipes that call for a springform pan call for a 9-inch (23-cm) pan, and this pan is used for no-bake cheesecakes and pies. You can even make my tart recipes in a springform pan. If you own an 8-inch (20-cm) pan, it can still be used for each recipe, but it may take additional time for the dessert to set since it will be thicker. If you have a 10-inch (25-cm) springform pan, you may need to adjust the amount of ingredients for the crust, and realize that your desserts will not be as tall as shown in my photos. Some desserts may need a little nudge to release them from the pan. I like to use my offset spatula or a flat-edged knife to slide around the inside edge of the pan.

TART PANS

Tart pans come in all shapes and sizes: round, rectangular, big, small and mini. Tart pans also have a removable edge so that once separated you are left with a beautifully scallop-edged dessert. Tart pans tend to hold less filling than a springform pan. I've tested my recipes in a variety of tart pan sizes, but most recipes can be made in a standard 9-inch (23-cm) tart pan. I also have recipes for mini-tart pans that are 4 inches (10 cm) and 6 inches (15 cm) in diameter. Be sure to press the crust tightly into the tart pan. Take caution when moving the tart pan around, since the bottom is removable. I like to put it on a small sheet pan to transport to and from the refrigerator. To remove the tart pan edge, hold the tart pan with both hands and gently push the bottom up at various points around the pan. Then, rest your pan on top of a round object smaller in diameter than your tart pan, and you will be able to easily remove the edges of the pan.

PIE PLATES

I chose not to prepare any desserts in a standard 9-inch (23-cm) pie plate because the crusts are not baked. Generally speaking, baking a graham cracker crust for 10 to 15 minutes will help maintain the integrity of the crust. This is why I prefer springform pans; you can easily have a beautiful crust without the extra fuss of baking. A few recipes I recommend trying in a pie plate would be the Bourbon Butterscotch Pudding Pie (page 53) and the Easy Chocolate Pudding Pie (page 63).

BAKING PANS

I have a variety of baking pans stocked in my kitchen cabinets. The most common ones you see in this book are the 8-inch (20-cm) square, 9-inch (23-cm) square and a typical brownie pan, which is 9 × 13-inch (23 × 33-cm). I have glass pans and metal pans, and since there is no baking required for this book, it doesn't matter if the pans are glass or metal. The one recommendation I have is that the sides be at least 2 ½ inches (6 cm) tall.

CUPCAKE PANS

I own more cupcake pans than I know what to do with. Over the years, I have narrowed them down to my favorite type and size and have discarded the other ones. For this cookbook, I only use cupcake pans to freeze ice cream treats. You will need a standard 12-cavity cupcake size and also a mini size, which usually has 24 cavities.

SILICONE BAKING MATS

I prefer to do all my baking on nonstick silicone baking mats. They come in very handy to line my brownie pans when I am preparing cheesecake or cookie bars as well. I also use them when I have any type of chocolate dipping to do for truffles. Once the chocolate has hardened, it is so easy to lift them right off the mat.

PARCHMENT PAPER

You'll notice I call for the use of parchment paper in many different places in this cookbook, but primarily as a lining for springform pans. I like to cut a square piece of parchment paper and place it on top of the bottom of the pan, and then I close the edges around the parchment paper. This works well when I remove the edges of my pan; it is much easier to actually lift the cheesecake off the base of the pan and transfer it to a plate or cake stand. I also like to buy precut parchment paper circles for my 9-inch (23-cm) pans. I buy those online or at a specialty cake supply store.

ALUMINUM FOIL

Similar to parchment paper, aluminum foil is very handy to wrap around the bottom of springform pans. It easily folds around the edges so that the springform edge can still be attached. I usually cover my desserts with aluminum foil prior to putting them in the refrigerator.

CLEAR PLASTIC WRAP

I know I am not the only one who rips out a sheet of clear plastic wrap and it shrinks and wrinkles and sticks to itself. However, clear plastic wrap is a necessary item for the kitchen. In this cookbook, I use it for all my pudding recipes. Placing the plastic wrap directly on the surface prevents a skin from forming on the top layer of the pudding.

STAND MIXER

My stand mixer is my life saver. I use it almost exclusively. I use both the whisk and paddle attachments. I mostly use the paddle attachment for my cheesecake and fillings. The whisk is needed for whipped cream. When I prepare whipped cream, I always freeze my metal bowl and sometimes the whisk. It is always best to mix your batter with a spatula before pouring it in the bowl. Dig down to the bottom of the bowl and turn it over to the top to help mix in any parts of the batter that did not get well mixed in.

HAND MIXER

A hand mixer is extremely useful in the kitchen. It is quickly accessible and easy to use. Hand mixers tend not to be as powerful as stand mixers, so generally speaking, you will need to mix the ingredients longer than specified in the recipe and scrape down the bowl more often.

FOOD PROCESSOR

Food processors are used for a variety of different functions. I have a food processor that has attachments of various sizes. I primarily use my food processor to grind the cookies or crackers into fine crumbs that are used for crusts.

MIXING BOWL

Mixing bowls come in various shapes and sizes. I own quite a few different ones, but all of them are metal or glass. I prefer metal bowls with a silicone base so they don't slide around on the counter. You'll want different sizes, and preferably a nesting set so they can be easily stored. Glass bowls are ideal for microwaving large batches of chocolate.

KITCHEN SCALE

I can't say enough about my kitchen scale. I don't have anything fancy, but I use it every single time I make anything that requires dry ingredients. Weighing dry ingredients is the key to successful baking. For some of my recipes, you will find a scale helpful for weighing ingredients such as chocolate and fruit.

OFFSET SPATULA

The offset spatula is my most prized kitchen tool. I use it on a regular basis, as often as I use a spatula. An offset spatula is an angled utensil with the flat-edged knife sitting lower than the handle. The flat edge is usually longer than the handle and has a rounded tip. It is ideal for spreading because it keeps your hand from getting in the way when you want a nice smooth surface, such as on the top of a cheesecake. I would recommend having at least 2 of these, and you might consider looking into various handy sizes.

MEASURING CUPS AND SPOONS

No kitchen is complete without measuring spoons. I have 2 sets of both measuring cups and spoons to help me with all of my baking. Having 2 sets means I usually do not have to wash them when I am in the middle of a recipe. I prefer my set that has a straight edge across the top for accurate measuring. My other set is angled and more difficult to ensure an even measurement.

COOKIE SCOOPS

I could never part ways with my beloved cookie scoops. I use them for filling cupcake batter, scooping mousse and whipped cream and, of course, scooping cookie dough. They really help maintain an even-size cookie.

ZESTER

I admit I had no idea what it means to own a good zester until I had one. I was using a fine cheese grater and it was doing what I needed it to do. I finally purchased a professional zester, and it has made a big difference! In case you aren't aware, zesting is removing the outside colored peel of a fruit. The zest is usually added to whatever you are cooking for flavor, and it sometimes is used as a garnish.

SIEVE

A sieve is a fine metal-mesh strainer. In this cookbook, a majority of my pudding recipes call for the pudding to be strained through a fine sieve to catch any ingredients that did not dissolve into the pudding.

WHISKS

I've done quite a bit of whisking in my day. I have both metal and silicone whisks, and I use them interchangeably. A metal whisk is typically more sturdy and best for thick batters. A silicone whisk is more flexible and great for whisking stove-top liquids because you can really dip your whisk into the bottom edges of the pan and pick up any remaining ingredients.

PASTRY (PIPING) BAG

I keep my pantry stocked with 2 sizes of durable pastry bags: 12 inches (30 cm) and 18 inches (46 cm). I always use the large pastry bag for piping whipped cream. I find that filling a piping bag is messy and difficult, so if I have all my batter or whipped cream in the bag at the beginning, I just need to worry about piping. Additionally, the large pastry bag is handy for filling mini-tarts, parfait cups and cupcake liners. The small pastry bags are most handy for adding the beautiful drizzle to the top of your dessert. You can use a sturdy plastic sandwich bag, but I find I can't get the tip to be fine enough for my liking.

PIPING TIPS

Man, I own a lot of piping tips, but you'll only need a couple for this cookbook. Have you ever wondered how bakeries get that perfect piping swirl that you can never master at home? It's because they are using jumbo piping tips. I use these for all of my whipped cream toppings and occasionally for my parfaits. My most commonly used piping tips are the Ateco 849 (closed star), 808 (open round), and 866 (Fresh star). You can find these online or at your local cake decorating store. Cut off the tip of your piping bag just above the opening of the tip and drop the tip right in.

FOOD COLORING

Just a couple recipes in this cookbook call for food coloring. I generally do not use a traditional liquid food coloring. Instead, I use gel colors. Gels are more concentrated so they have less liquid. Oftentimes you will need only a couple of drops of the gel to achieve your desired color. Since they contain less water, they do not dilute the thickness of your batter. Try brands such as Wilton or Amerigel. These can be purchased online or at your local craft or baking store.

USEFUL INGREDIENTS

BUTTER

All recipes in this book are prepared with unsalted butter, which I use exclusively in my kitchen when it comes to baking, or, in this case, no-bake desserts. Unsalted butter allows the flavors to shine through without affecting the salt content. I use butter most commonly for crusts.

CAKE MIX

A couple of recipes in this book call for dry cake mix, brownie mix or hot chocolate powder. You only need to open the bag, measure out the necessary amount, and add it to the batter. That is why it is specified as dry powder.

CHOCOLATE

It goes without saying, the better the quality of chocolate, the better the taste. However, the taste also depends on the amount of cocoa powder and additives in the chocolate. This is especially true for white chocolate. I never use store-brand white chocolate. It usually does not get nearly as smooth as it needs to, and it often produces a oilier ganache, which affects the texture of the dessert. You'll notice that I often call for dark chocolate, which is my preferred chocolate. Feel free to use milk chocolate if that is what you prefer.

I use chocolate in a variety of ways in this cookbook. Sometimes it's melted and mixed into the dessert; sometimes it's chopped up and added to the finished product; sometimes it's a garnish. I also use it for dipping, which you can read more about in the Candy Dipping section (page 210).

COCOA POWDER

Just like chocolate, cocoa powder comes in a number of varieties. I always buy high-quality cocoa powder as this often gives the best results. There are different types of cocoa powder, but I tend to stick with sweetened and unsweetened. Sweetened cocoa powder is less bitter because it contains added sugar. It is not as common as unsweetened cocoa powder. I use both in my kitchen, but the recipes in this book call for unsweetened cocoa powder as it is more readily available.

CREAM CHEESE

Different brands of cream cheese perform differently. I notice that most store-bought brands seem more watery and lack the creamy flavor I am used to. My preferred brand is Philadelphia. All recipes in this book use full-fat cream cheese. I do not use low-fat or fat-free cream cheese because I do not like the results they produce, and if I am going to eat dessert, I am going to do it all the way! I often start with whipping the heck out of the cream cheese so it is nice and fluffy, and I find it is easier to do that with cold cream cheese. However, I find that most people are more comfortable using softened cream cheese. If you do need to soften cream cheese, remove the wrapper and microwave for 15 to 30 seconds.

EGGS

You'll find that eggs are used in all my recipes that contain homemade pudding. All of these recipes call for large eggs, as they are the most common size used in baking.

ESPRESSO POWDER

I prefer to make all coffee flavored desserts with espresso powder as it produces a very strong brewed coffee when combined with water. This is a common ingredient found with ground or instant coffee in grocery stores. If you are unable to locate espresso powder, substitute with a strong brewed coffee.

FLOUR

A few of my recipes call for flour. I use standard all-purpose white flour. Most recipes that call for flour call for only a small amount, so there is no reason to sift the flour.

HOT FUDGE AND CARAMEL SAUCE

I cannot even count the number of recipes that call for either hot fudge or caramel sauce. It is used mostly as a garnish but occasionally it is added to a recipe. I like to use a brand name such as Hershey's, Ghirardelli or Smuckers. As I said in the Choosing a Garnish section (page 208), hot fudge sauce makes the most perfect topping to drizzle over slices of cheesecake, a parfait or a tart.

MALT POWDER

Malted milk powder is an ingredient commonly found alongside hot chocolate or powdered chocolate milk mixes. It is a popular additive to milkshakes and is used for ice cream in this cookbook.

MARSHMALLOW CRÈME

Several recipes in this book use marshmallow crème. In my cheesecake, the marshmallow crème adds an unbelievable airiness to the dessert. The most common brand I use is Jet-Puffed.

MILK

Occasionally, my pudding recipes call for milk. In my house, we only drink nonfat milk, which is what I used in these recipes. However, you can use whatever milk you wish. If you use whole milk, you might find that your pudding is thicker.

PEANUT BUTTER

While I love peanut butter, I tend not to keep it in my pantry because it's so addicting! The recipes in this book use a standard creamy peanut butter such as Jif or Skippy. I suggest not using a fancy peanut butter that requires mixing, because it has more oil.

PUMPKIN

My love for pumpkin started at an early age, and I am sharing my passion with you in a couple of my recipes. I use canned pumpkin puree such as Libbys. Do not use canned pumpkin pie mix.

SUGAR

You'll find a variety of sugars used in this cookbook, primarily granulated, powdered and light brown sugar. While I use a scale to measure almost all dry ingredients, you can get by without it. Brown sugar should always be packed into your measuring cup. Granulated and powdered sugar can be scooped and leveled off by shaking the measuring cup back and forth. Again, I prefer using brand name sugar, especially powdered sugar because it tends to contain less corn starch than store brands. A professional cake maker told me this very early on and I won't forget it!

SWEETENED CONDENSED MILK

I always use full-fat sweetened condensed milk in my recipes. This is a great ingredient for no-churn ice cream and homemade pudding.

VANILLA EXTRACT

I go through vanilla extract like it's nobody's business. While I always recommend using a good vanilla extract, it needs to at least be a pure vanilla extract and not imitation. You can purchase high-quality brands such as Nielsen-Massey, which I love, but for most standard baking, I use McCormick as it is most readily available.

acknowledgments

It is so surreal to be sitting here writing the acknowledgments for my very first cookbook. My first freaking cookbook! I never thought 2016 would give me such an opportunity. People often ask me when I am going to open a bakery or write a cookbook. Only one of those have I ever even considered. The process of creating this cookbook was no simple task, and it took an army of people to get me through it.

First, I would like to thank the love of my life, Kevin. From day one you've supported me, encouraged me, lifted me up when I was doubting myself, wiped away my tears and celebrated my milestones. Thank you for your everlasting patience, even when there was not a single spot left in the refrigerator.

I don't really know if I will ever be able to show my parents how truly thankful I am for their endless encouragement to work hard and follow my dreams. To my dad, who came cross-country to wash dishes, make desserts and, of course, to eat them too, I can't thank you enough for the endless hours of editing and helping me get through the final days. To my mom, who helped me come up with ideas, tested recipes and offered to help in any way she could, I am forever thankful to you both.

I have too many friends and family around the country to mention. From Santa Barbara to Vermont, thank you all for encouraging me and for celebrating right along with me. The leftover desserts help, I'm sure.

To my loyal readers of Beyond Frosting, this book is for you! I'm not sure I would be able to put up with all of the craziness in my life if it weren't for your support. I so much appreciate all of your comments, emails, tweets and pins. Thank you for sharing my recipes with your family and friends, and then coming back for more. So many of you signed up to test recipes for my book, whether it was 2 or 5, you guys are incredible. Thank you for making this book a success.

A special thank you to all my blogging friends who encouraged me, talked me through my craziness, and helped me test recipes for this book. Blogging would not be the same without you. I am so thankful we've met through this crazy Internet world. To Lindsay, there is no one else I would want to go through this process with. I can't wait to see our books on the shelves together!

This book would not be possible without the editorial team at Page Street. Thank you for taking a chance on me, allowing me to pursue my passion and answering my endless questions.

Lastly, a sincere thanks to all of *you* for getting a copy of my book. I hope you enjoy these desserts as much as I do.

XO, Julianne

about the author

Julianne Bayer is the author of the sugar-packed baking blog Beyond Frosting. She is a Vermont transplant living in Southern California. Between winters on the slopes, Julianne spends time baking, creating and, of course, tasting all types of desserts. Julianne works full-time in the action-sports industry and spends evenings and weekends in the kitchen working on her baking addiction. She still finds time to snowboard as much as possible.

After taking cake decorating classes, Julianne quickly realized that she missed being in the kitchen. As a child, she had always enjoyed helping her mother and grandmothers bake, host parties and share their treats. Fast forward to 2012. Julianne launched Beyond Frosting with the goal of sharing her recipes and inspiring others to get baking. She believes memories are created in the kitchen and hopes others will fall madly in love with the experience of creating unique desserts.

Julianne's recipes have been featured on popular websites such as Better Homes and Gardens, Cosmopolitan, Country Living, Good Housekeeping, Delish, Redbook, The Kitchn, Huffington Post, Buzzfeed and King Arthur Flour. She has also been featured in publications from *Better Homes and Gardens*, *Cake Central Magazine* and *Sift*.

You can find more from Julianne online at beyondfrosting.com.

ndex